E   F

RESTEN

Kainzen

1

H

B 319

2

Buchenhöhe

22

H

20

H

Klaushöhe

3

LAROSBACH

Kehlstein

Obere Kehlalm

23

"Kehlsteinhaus"
(1837)

24

← OBERSALZBERG

Kehlsteinstr. (Bus connection only)

KEHLSTEIN

4

E   F

PROLOGUE The Berchtesgaden Land and the Obersalzberg are among the most beautiful German countrysides. Thousands of tourists visit this spot every year. Some of the most special sights are the Königssee with the world-renowned St. Bartholomä peninsula or the unique Berchtesgaden National Park. Many visitors also come for their interest in the vivid history of the region. This "Past Finder® Obersalzberg 1933–1945" aims to give objective and critical information about those times when Berchtesgaden was, along with Munich, Berlin, and Nuremberg, one of the most important power centres of the expanded German "Reich". This specialized guide offers additions to the existing literature. It does not attempt in any way to reduce the history of the region to those twelve dramatic years.

HOW TO USE THE PAST FINDER

Colour-coded bars with chapter headings at the top of the page take you to the respective maps for the area specified in the bar. On the map, the numbered items in the text section are placed in the respective reference grid. The individual description of a building or site first explains its use during the Nazi period, and, if the building has survived, its current function.

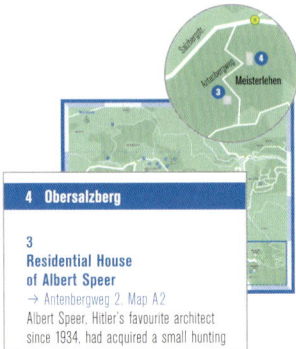

LEGEND

⌂ Architect and year of construction
  Address and grid reference on
  the map of the same colour
🕐 Opening times
▷ Reference to index

FINDING YOUR WAY ON THE OBERSALZBERG

The Obersalzberg was totally annihilated by the Nazis; the British air raid of April 1945 in its turn destroyed a great part of the Nazi buildings. Few houses have survived this history. The Obersalzberg Documentation Centre stands at the site of the former Guesthouse of the Nazi party. Another point of orientation has been added in recent years with the "InterContinental Resort" hotel.

Tourist Information

→ Berchtesgaden Directorate of Tourism (Kurdirektion), Königseer Str. 2, Berchtesgaden
🕐 Mon–Fri 8.30–17, Sat 9–12
→ Kur- and Kongresshaus, Maximilianstr. 9, Berchtesgaden
🕐 Mon–Fri 8.30–17, Sat 9–12

Public Transportation

Information about bus transport of the Regionalverkehr Oberbayern GmbH is available at every bus stop. Information and tickets for the regional and long distance connections of the Deutsche Bahn are available at the Main Railway Station in Berchtesgaden.

PASTFINDER OBERSALZBERG

CH. LINKS VERLAG, BERLIN

12 Hitler's "Berghof" on the Obersalzberg, 1936. Background: Hoher Göll (2,523 metre)

OBERSALZBERG Toward the end of the 19th century, the village of Obersalzberg was a favourite rehabilitation site. It owed this reputation to its climate. After Hitler had become Reich Chancellor in 1933 and had acquired House "Wachenfeld", Martin Bormann brutally expelled the inhabitants. Some of them had lived for generations at Obersalzberg. Hitler had his vacation house expanded into the pompous "Berghof". Other prominent National Socialists followed his example. Systematically the Nazis exploited the region and turned it into a strongly guarded second seat of government. SS Barracks, the spectacular "Kehlsteinhaus", and an expansive Shelter System were built. The end of the war, however, happened in Hitler's absence from Obersalzberg. He had committed suicide in the "Führerbunker" in Berlin.

1
Estate of Martin Bormann/ Golf Club Berchtesgaden
⌂ 1940 → Salzbergstraße 33, Map A2
The former Estate of the Head of the Party Chancellery and private secretary to the "Führer", Martin Bormann, is today one of the last visible mega-construction projects of the Nazis on the Obersalzberg. Totally erased from view, however, were the traces of the community of Obersalzberg, which had developed since the middle of the 19th century. The village stood as an obstacle to Hitler's construction plans. Bormann made sure that the historic inhabitants were driven out and that their properties were destroyed or burnt. The last active farmers had to leave Obersalzberg in the beginning of 1937. Shortly afterwards Bormann noted in his calendar: **"The Führer agrees to the plans for the new Estate."**
The expansive facility was planned according to the most modern standards and built with great technical effort. The farm included stables for cows and horses, a facility for fattening pigs, cold storage houses for milk, a beehive and a three-storey administrative building. An agronomist was responsible for the Estate (there was a second farm in Mecklenburg). Constant subventions were needed due to the immense construction costs and the poor farm yields. The regime propaganda nonetheless advertised the premises as a "model farm" for the planned colonization of the occupied territories in the East.

During the war, workers had to dig the so-called Estate underground shelter a total of 1,1 km into the neighbouring Antenberg. After 50 metres, one of the shelter tunnels opens into a gigantic seven-metre high hall. There a cavern, made inhabitable, served Bormann's employees and the neighbouring family Speer as air raid shelter. During post-war times, the US army used the Estate as "Skytop Lodge", a sports hotel with a golf course and ski lift. Today, the construction ensemble and its expansive grounds are home to the Golf Club Berchtesgaden.

2
Teahouse
⌂ Roderich Fick, 1937 → Mooslahner-kopf, Map B1 The Teahouse, a little pavilion on the Mooslahnerkopf, not far from the ▷ Estate, was built in 1937. At its centre, a circular room with underfloor heating held a big round table seating eight persons. From this spot, a panorama window offered a view over the Berchtesgaden valley. Hitler came here frequently during his extensive afternoon walks. In contrast to the ▷ **"Kehlsteinhaus"**, this Teahouse served exclusively private purposes. The "Führer" allowed the engineer Ferdinand Porsche to join him on the Mooslahnerkopf, as well as the Mercedes Benz sales manager Jakob Werlin, the architect Albert Speer and the national sculptor Josef Thorak, among others. In 1952 the building was demolished except for a few remains.

3
Residential House
of Albert Speer
→ Antenbergweg 2, Map A2

Albert Speer, Hitler's favourite architect since 1934, had acquired a small hunting lodge at Ostertal in the Bavarian Alps at the beginning of 1935, to serve him as studio during vacation times. He wanted to spend more time with his family here and concurrently work on the countless construction projects Hitler had assigned him in pleasant surroundings with the team from his architecture office.

When Hitler heard of this, he offered Speer the former residence of the artist Waltenberger on the Obersalzberg instead. Speer accepted with pleasure the invitation to advance into the private circle around Hitler, alongside Eva Braun, Martin Bormann and Hermann Göring. Soon, the premises turned out to be too small for his family and employees of the architecture office, and he started with sketches for a separate ▷ **Studio** in the immediate vicinity.

After the war, the US army used the residence as an exclusive Guesthouse for officers. Today it is private property.

4
Studio of Albert Speer
⌂ Albert Speer, 1938 → Antenberg-weg 1, Map A2 The building, which was designed by Speer himself, served the architect of the "Führer" as a residence and studio. It meant that he was even able to discuss the countless construction projects he was assigned with the "Führer" during the times of Hitler's frequent vacation on Obersalzberg.

Appointed "Inspector General of Building for the Reich Capital" in 1937, Speer was responsible for the entire construction planning which was to turn Berlin into the future world capital "Germania". Together, Hitler and Speer often sat here in front of the monumental construction models. After the war, the US army confiscated the studio and used it as conference building under the name "Evergreen Lodge". The house had survived the war undamaged and is now private property.

5
"Kampfhäusl" (Fighting Hut)
→ Salzbergstraße, Map B2 After Hitler had tried in vain to seize government power through a putsch on 8–9 November 1923, he was incarcerated in Landsberg am Lech. There he wrote the first part of his book "Mein Kampf" before he was prematurely released at Christmas 1924 after only eight months of prison. In 1925 he sought accommodation incognito as "Mr. Wolf" on Obersalzberg, which his mentor Dietrich Eckart had recommended to him, to dictate the second volume of "Mein Kampf" to his fellow party member Max Amann.

The owner of the ▷ **Hotel "Platterhof"**, Bruno Büchner, gave him a small wooden hut above Obersalzbergstraße for this purpose. This hut served Hitler until 1927 as a dictation room and a hiding place from the government forces of Bavaria, which had banned him from speaking in public.

The Nazi propaganda later called the hut the "Kampfhäusl". The only remains are the wildly overgrown stone foundations of the building demolished in 1952.

6
Theatre Hall
⌂ Ludwig Hilz, Friedrich Haindl, 1937 → Antenberg, Map B3 The Theatre Hall was built in 1937 as a cinema and function room for the workers of Obersalzberg, with a capacity of up to 2,000 persons. As late as 20 April 1945, Hitler's last birthday, an NSDAP Local Chapter was founded here. Former District Leader (Gauleiter) in Munich Paul Giesler, who had fled here, declared that he drew new courage and belief **"from the site of the holy mountain"**. Area Leader (Kreisleiter) Stredele added: **"There will still be a miracle. Hitler himself will be the miracle."** A few days later, Hitler committed suicide in Berlin. Giesler followed the example of his "Führer" and committed suicide on 3 May 1945 in Berchtesgaden. The Theatre Hall was taken down and erected in Munich as the Jesus' Heart Church (Herz-Jesu-Kirche). It burnt down in 1994. Its concrete foundations can still be seen on Obersalzberg today.

4 Hitler and Albert Speer examining architecture plans in the studio, 1935

1 Exit gate of Bormann's Estate

4 Speer's Studio, 1939

1 Stables on Bormann's Estate

3 Albert Speer's first Residential House

6 Concrete foundations of the Theatre Hall, 2005

A Village Is Razed to the Ground

At the end of the 19th century the upper Bavarian farming village of Obersalzberg advanced to the status of a favourite convalescence site due to its healthy climate. Prominent and wealthy guests

Demolition of houses while still inhabited

included the pianist Clara Schumann and the psychoanalyst Sigmund Freud. Industrialists such as Carl v. Linde or Arthur Eichengrün, who had developed Aspirin for "Bayer", also acquired small summer residences here.

Adolf Hitler came to Obersalzberg for the first time in the spring of 1923. Ten years later he was Reich Chancellor, and able to buy the ▷ **House "Wachenfeld"** he had previously rented. The modest vacation house was soon remodelled into a pompous ▷ **"Berghof".** The longstanding local inhabitants were now in his way. Hitler's right-hand man, Martin Bormann, was put in charge of the dirty job of getting rid of them. Without scruples, he fulfilled his "Führer's" wishes.

Karl Schuster, the owner of the ▷ **Hotel "Zum Türken",** was to become one of the first victims of the new neighbours. From the time Hitler had moved in on the lower side of the hotel, hundreds of curious spectators came to see the "Führer". The hotel's garden therefore offered the ideal viewing platform. With time, however, Schuster disapproved of this circus. When SS and SA men held a loud drinking binge on his premises he complained: **"Is there nobody else here any more than blacks and browns (Nazis)? It's like living in a penitentiary here."** The Nazis immediately responded. On Hitler's command, the ▷ **Hotel "Zum Türken"** was boycotted with posters and watchmen from 18 August 1933 on. All guests and employees had to leave the building. Schuster was taken into "protective arrest" for two weeks. Eventually, Bormann forced the family to sell the property, paid the comparatively appropriate sum of 150,000 Reichsmark, and decreed that they vacate the premises within eight days. The SS stood guard to make sure they took only a few clothes and personal documents. In a newspaper announcement, the Local NSDAP Chapter threatened arrest in the Dachau concentration camp for anybody who talked about the fate of the Schusters in public. After the hotel "Zum Türken", the owner

Chapel "Maria Hilf" and the Dr. Seitz Paediatric Sanatorium, Bormann's later Residential House

of the ▷ **Hotel "Platterhof"** and the owner of the newly renovated Alpine Guesthouse "Steiner" were forced to sell. In these cases, however, the price was far below the value of the properties. The remainder of the Obersalzberg citizens were to leave their homes in the winter of 1936/37. Without delay, Bormann had their roofs taken off. **"Taking down the houses was done with utmost expediency to save the Führer the ugly sight of the demolition sites"**, Bormann commented in his notes.

One of the most obstinate Obersalzberg citizens was Josef Hölzl, the owner of the "Oberwurflehen". He had not sold his property by October 1936 and had even ignored a final ultimatum. Finally, Bormann showed up in person at the beginning of 1937 and threatened him with a concentration camp.
A few days later, in the presence of two Gestapo men, Hölzl had to sign the sale

"You do not need to sell the house, but then you will receive nothing and you will go to concentration camp." (Martin Bormann to Josef Hölzl, 1937)

contract. He received 1 Reichsmark per square metre for the house, and not a penny for the forest next to it.
Meanwhile, even the tiny catholic chapel "Maria Hilf" had disappeared from the village, and the former children's sanatorium "Dr. Seitz" now served Bormann as residence. Immediately beneath the ▷ **"Berghof"** the only buildings left in Hitler's view were the farmhouses of Josef Rasp and of the Bomhardt family. After Rasp had died at the age of 78, Bormann promptly declared the farm in need of demolition and had the premises forcibly cleared within 24 hours.

With Hitler's consent, Bormann had a total of 50 houses demolished in Obersalzberg. Some of those were farms that had been family properties for hundreds of years.

Martin Bormann 1900–1945

Marin Bormann was born in Halberstadt on 17 June 1900. During his apprenticeship as a farmer, he first came into contact with radical rightwing groups. Because of his participation in a hate murder, he was convicted to one year in prison in 1924 together with the later commander of the Auschwitz concentration camp, Rudolf Höß. He became a member of the NSDAP in 1927 and cleverly worked his way up to the centre of power. From 1933 on he no longer left Hitler's side, as Reich Leader. He represented the ideas of his "Führer" with administrative efficiency and brutality. Among the first victims of his totalitarian politics were the citizens of Obersalzberg. As Head of the Party Chancellery and secretary to the "Führer", besides his aggression against the churches, he was predominantly active in the domain of "race politics". Factually Hitler's representative from 1943 on, Bormann forced the deportation of the Jewish population of Germany and of the occupied territories into the SS death camps for total annihilation. After Hitler's suicide in the "Führerbunker", Bormann escaped from the government district under attack. He disappeared without leaving a trace. During excavations at Berlin's Lehrter Bahnhof (today: Hauptbahnhof) in 1972, his skeleton was found. After a failed attempt at escape, he had poisoned himself.

Bormann's oldest son Martin is an active opponent of right wing radicalism. As a priest and theology teacher, he holds talks all over Germany about the Nazi era. After several visits to Israel, he became a member of the Persecutor Victim Group (Täter-Opfer-Gruppe) founded by Dan Bar-On (TRT – to reflect and trust).

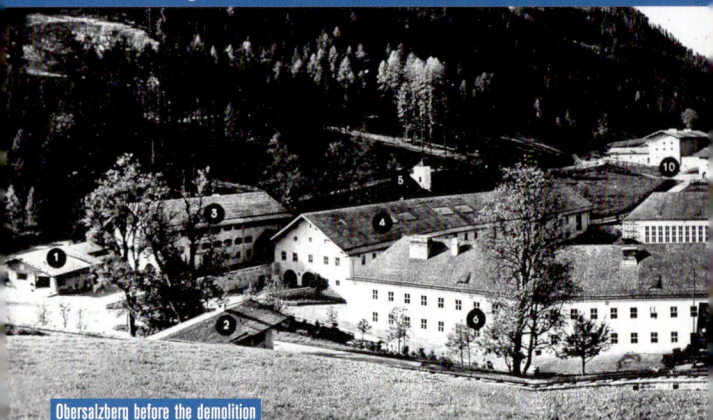

Obersalzberg before the demolition

1. Post Office in the restricted zone 2. Gardening building 3. Drivers' residence
7. Barracks, Leibstandarte exercise hall 8. Barracks square, basements with shooting stands
12. Administration Obersalzberg 13. Model building for architectural planning 14. Kindergarten

Mega-Construction Site Obersalzberg

7
Shelter Camp Antenberg

→ Antenberg, Map B2 While traces
of the ▷ SS Barracks or the ▷ Hotel
"Platterhof" have largely disappeared, the
forests of the area still hold numerous
relics of the former Mega-Construction
Site Obersalzberg. Here, at Antenberg,
one finds remainders of former foreign
and forced labour camps. At times, up to
6,000 manual and other labourers worked
on the Nazis' construction projects on
the Obersalzberg. Until the beginning of
the war, there was still a predominantly
German workforce, along with some
Italian and Austrian professional special-
ists who were paid according to tariff.
Additionally, they were paid a 50 Pfennig
per day Obersalzberg bonus.
Later, ever more forced labourers from
Poland and the Czech Republic were
used.
The "workers from the east" ranked at
the bottom of the Nazi hierarchy. They
barely received food. Their clothes were
absolutely unfit. On top of that they were
frequently mistreated. They were housed
in primitive wooden Barracks, guarded
by the SS or German foremen.
To prevent sexual contact between the
"workers from the east" and the local
population, here – as everywhere else
in the Reich – special brothel Barracks
were established, where female concentration camp prisoners had to perform
"services".

8
Hotel "Platterhof"

⌂ Roderich Fick, 1937 → Salzbergstraße 45, Map C2 The opening of the
Guesthouse "Moritz" by Mauritia Mayer
in 1877 was the beginning of the devel-
opment of tourism on the Obersalzberg.
The hotel was sold in 1919. The new
leaseholder Bruno Büchner named the
Guesthouse "Platterhof". In May 1923 a
certain Mr. Wolf alias Adolf Hitler arrived
on Obersalzberg. At the "Platterhof" he
visited Dietrich Eckart alias Dr. Hoffmann,
who was a Nazi lyricist and editor of
the "Völkischer Beobachter" newspaper,
among other occupations. Eckart was
wanted by the police for his violation of
the Protection of the Republic Act (Repu-
blikschutzgesetz) and living incognito.

8 Ballroom of the Hotel "Platterhof", 2005

4. Parking garage 5. Gatehouse to the restricted zone 6. Barracks, administrative building
9. Barracks, living quarters 10. Guesthouse "Platterhof" 11. Residence for "Platterhof" employees
15. "Berghotel" 16. Reich Security Service and Gestapo

After the forced sale of the "Platterhof" to the NSDAP, the modest Guesthouse was expanded into a spacious hotel building in 1936.

The new construction had to circumvent Dietrich Eckart's room, which had become a memorial site. Martin Bormann wanted to make the hotel "Platterhof" into a people's hotel. As part of the "Strength through Joy" programme, one night's stay was to cost 1 Reichsmark per person. From the beginning of the Second World War in 1939, wounded German soldiers were roomed here. The US Army used the "Platterhof" during post-war times as the "General Walker Hotel".

The German authorities ordered demolition of the whole complex in the year 2000. Only a small festival room remains on Salzbergstraße.

9
SS Barracks

⌂ Roderich Fick, 1937 → Salzbergstraße 45. Map C2 SS Barracks were constructed in closest proximity to Adolf Hitler's ▷ **"Berghof"** in 1937. The premises consisted of four about 100-metre-long buildings around a parade ground: one building for living quarters, one for management of the premises, one for sports and one large garage. In underground firearms facilities, members of the "Schwarzer Orden" were trained in the use of weapons. By the end of the war, the SS commando "Obersalzberg" numbered 2,265 men. Among those were Hitler's Fahrkolonne, an SS guard company, the fire fighter police, an SS flak and fog division, as well as an SS tunnel construction company. From 1943, the commander was SS Obersturmbannführer

9 During the presentation of new uniforms, Major General Stieff (2nd r.) was to detonate a bomb close to Hitler

Documentation Centre

Dr. Bernhard Frank. In June of 1943 the latest weapons for the ▷ **Mountain Infantry** were put on show on the parade ground in front of the Barracks in the presence of Hitler and the aviation constructor Heinrich Focke. A Focke-Wulf Fa 223 carrier helicopter was introduced, along with a Mercedes Benz UNIMOG with an integrated mountain howitzer and new uniforms. Major General Helmuth Stieff was also present. Along with Claus Schenk, Count of Stauffenberg, he was one of the military conspirers who had decided to oppose and kill Hitler in order to end the war. Stauffenberg had hoped that Stieff would be able to explode a bomb in front of Hitler on the Obersalzberg on that day or at ▷ **Kleßheim Castle** on 7 July. But when given the detonation materials, Stieff suddenly did not want to get involved. This remained one of a dozen unachieved plans for attempt on Hitler's life.

The Barracks were destroyed during British air raids on 25 April 1945. In 2002 the remaining basement premises were cleared out of rubble and filled in.

10
Party Chancellery and Party Guesthouse "Hoher Göll"/Obersalzberg Documentation Centre
⌂ Alois Degano, 1935 → Salzbergstraße 41, Map B2 ⊙ Apr–Oct Mon–Sun 9–17, Nov–March Tue–Sun 10–15

The party Guesthouse "Hoher Göll" was originally part of the pension "Moritz". Together with the neighbouring ▷ **Hotel "Platterhof"**, it was remodelled and expanded at great expense in 1935. High-ranking foreign dignitaries were to stay here. Predominantly, however, it served as an administrative building for the Head of the Party Chancellery Martin Bormann.

After the war, the barely damaged house stood empty and decayed. Shortly after the departure of the US troops the Bavarian government decided to build a documentation centre on the Obersalzberg in 1995. On 20 October 1999 the permanent exhibition was opened, designed by the Munich Institute of Contemporary History. During the main season, the centre attracts an average of 120,000 visitors, and the tendency is rising. The exhibition centers on the history of the Obersalzberg and sets out the Nazi terror regime as a whole. Additionally, parts of the underground ▷ **Shelter System** are accessible for visitors.

11
Hotel "Zum Türken", Headquarters of the Reich Security Service
⌂ 1911 → Hintereck, Map C2 The origins of the hotel and restaurant "Zum Türken" reach back into the year 1630. According to local legend, the name comes from the owner of the time who had returned from the war against Turkey in 1683 and who was called "der Türke" or "the Turk" from then on. In 1903 Karl Schuster bought the premises and opened the hotel "Zum Türken". After the family had been forced to sell the property by Martin Bormann, a part of the "Leibstandarte SS Adolf Hitler" and 30 bodyguards from the Reich Security Service (RSD – Reichssicherheitsdienst) were stationed here from mid 1934 on for Hitler's protection. Hitler's personal security was under the responsibility of SS General Johann Rattenhuber. The RSD on the Obersalzberg encompassed 250 men in 1944. They were in charge of the supervision of all postal and telephone communications. In the basement, on top of the tunnels of the ▷ **Shelter System,** the RSD had prison cells for arrests. The building was heavily damaged during British air raids on 25 April 1945, then looted. In 1949 Karl Schuster's daughter Therese filed for restitution of her property and was the only previous Obersalzberg citizen to receive her former property, the hotel and restaurant, back from the Bavarian Free State. Today, the hotel "Zum Türken" is once again a favourite spot on the Obersalzberg; its proximity to the remains of Hitler's ▷ **"Berghof"** is not the least of the reasons.

10 Obersalzberg Documentation Centre

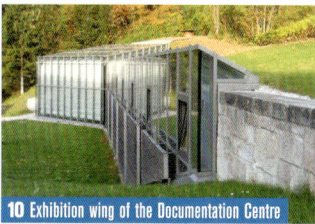

10 Exhibition wing of the Documentation Centre

10 Painting of the "Berghof" in the Documentation Centre

10 Exhibition hall in the Obersalzberg Documentation Centre

10 Entry to the Shelter System

11 Hotel "Zum Türken" with former SS Guardhouse

Hitler's "Berghof"

12

House "Wachenfeld", "Berghof"

⌂ 1916, 1938, Alois Degano → Hintereck, Map C2 House "Wachenfeld" was built in 1916 for the dealer with leather goods Otto Winter of Buxtehude. The small vacation domicile below the the new construction. East of its front was a long stretched annex built for the adjutants and servants next to the main building. Behind the main building was another wing with offices and a complete dental practice. The showpiece of the

12 Hitler's Office

12 Panorama window with globe

▷ Hotel "Zum Türken" was named after his wife, born Wachenfeld. Hitler presumably rented the house for the first time in spring 1927. He finally bought it for 40,000 Reichsmark in the summer of 1933. With Hitler being Reich Chancellor, life on the Obersalzberg changed drastically. The small village became off-limits for the general public ("Führersperrgebiet") and was taken over by other Nazi functionaries such as Martin Bormann, Hermann Göring and Albert Speer.

Based on Hitler's sketches, house "Wachenfeld" was converted into the much larger "Berghof" in 1936. After completion of the works, the old house "Wachenfeld" was totally absorbed by "Berghof" was the "great hall" in the main building with its 285 square-metre area. A panorama window, 9 metre by 3,60 metre with a mechanism for lowering it into the frame, gave a beautiful view of the mountain scenery. In unfavourable weather conditions, however, intensive exhaust gas entered the window from Hitler's automobile park underneath it. A five-metre table for maps was used for strategic discussions with the military during the war. Next to it stood a big globe. On it, it is said that Hitler had marked the preliminary target of his attack on Russia: the Archangelsk–Astrakhan line – a line along the Ural Mountain from the Barents Sea up to the Caspian Sea.

12 Access driveway to Hitler's "Berghof", 1936

Gerdy Troost, the widow of the deceased first "Architect of the Führer" Paul Ludwig Troost, was responsible for the overall conception of the interior design of the "Berghof". Huge 18thcentury Flemish tapestries covered the walls of the big living hall. They could be pulled aside for the many movie viewings. A seating area in front offered Hitler and his guests ample space. Among others, movie presentations included UFA productions,

through the Reich Security Service. Still, an attempt on Hitler's life had been planned even at the "Berghof". Before Claus von Stauffenberg set off his bomb in the "Wolfsschanze" Führer Headquarters near Rastenburg in Poland on 20 July 1944, the cavalry captain Eberhard von Breitenbach had decided to shoot the dictator. As an adjutant to General Busch, he was to participate in strategic talks on the Obersalzberg on

12 Hitler in parade uniform

12 Remains of the "Berghof", 2005

Charlie Chaplin films and some Mickey Mouse cartoons, and the latest weekly news reports. Hitler's office was on the upper floor. This was the site of talks with the British Prime Minister Chamberlain, the Austrian Chancellor Schuschnigg, or during the Second World

"Yes, I am deeply connected with the mountain (...). Much has happened there, came about and passed, those are among the most beautiful times of my life. All my great plans were born there." (Adolf Hitler)

War with leaders of the vassal states. Hitler's bedroom was separated by the bathroom and dressing rooms from the adjacent room of Eva Braun. His secret lover was not allowed to be seen during visits of dignitaries. True to the propaganda of the self-controlled "Führer" who sacrifices himself for the people of his country, his only official "bride" was called Germany.

Alarm buttons in all rooms of the "Berghof" served the security of the dictator. Food was analysed chemically before preparing meals, mail and clean laundry was put through an x-ray

11 March 1944. In the outer entrance room to the "Berghof", von Breitenbach handed in his professional weapon as expected, while he kept a second firearm hidden in his uniform. But on that exact day, adjutants had no access to the strategic talks with Hitler. Over three hours, Eberhard von Breitenbach sat in the front room with a loaded weapon, before he was able to leave for his return trip.

Hitler's last will stipulated that the "Berghof" was the property of the German Reich. That will materialized as little as the planned extension of the premises into a palace-like residence. After the British bombing raid on 25 April 1945 and the detonations of the charred "Berghof" ruin, few vestiges are left over today. Not far from the ▷ **Obersalzberg Documentation Centre,** the solid supporting walls of the rear of the "Berghof" protrude from the mountain slope. Underground are the inaccessible basement and shelter rooms of Hitler's "Berghof" including his private bowling lanes. Every now and then funeral candles left by Neo-Nazis and swastikas cut into trees point to the historical significance of this crime scene. Purposefully, no explanatory plaque with directions was erected here.

Adolf Hitler 1889–1945

"I was born in Braunau am Inn on 20 April 1889 as the son of the local postal official Alois Hitler. My total education encompasses 5 classes of primary school and 4 classes of lower secondary school. One goal of my youth was to become a master builder, and I do not think that if politics had not taken hold of me I would ever have turned to any other profession," wrote Hitler toward the end of 1921 in his vita. After the death of his parents in 1907 he had moved to Vienna and lived off his little inheritance and as a postcard painter. He applied to study at the Academy of Arts in vain. After reading anti-semitic writings he developed a keen enmity to Marxism, Liberalism and Judaism.

The beginning of the First World War brought a decisive turning point in Hitler's unglamorous life. He volunteered for the Bavarian infantry. Awarded the Iron Cross, first and second class, he experienced the German capitulation while lying in an army hospital.

Afterwards Hitler worked as a whistle-blower for the political army intelligence service in Munich and joined the German Worker's Party (DAP – Deutsche Arbeiter-partei). Under his leadership the party, meanwhile renamed the NSDAP (Natio-nalsozialistische Deutsche Arbeiterpartei), gained a considerable voter potential during the early 20s in Bavaria. Hitler's attempt to overthrow the democracy of Weimar with a putsch against the government in November 1923 ended with his arrest. After his premature release, the NSDAP had been reestablished in 1925 and established itself as the strongest faction in the Reichstag by 1932. On 30 January 1933 Hitler was appointed Reich Chancellor.

With his surprise attack on Poland on 1 September 1939, Hitler unchained the forces which began the Second World War. After further victories over half of Europe, critical voices went silent. Only the defeat at Stalingrad brought a turn-around in 1943, with the war returning "home to the Reich" shortly afterwards.

Hitler had the lifelong conviction that, like his parents, he was destined to die young. In fact, seven years of war had physically brought the dictator to his knees. "Patient A" as the medics called him, suffered from cardiac insufficiency, strong stomach cramps and he had Parkinson's Disease from 1944 on. His paladins had still hoped to get the "Führer" out of Berlin around which the battle raged and to fly him to the ▷ **Alpine Fortress.** But Hitler eventually chose to die in Berlin. After his marriage to Eva Brown, the couple committed suicide together on 30 April 1945. Their corpses were burnt beyond recognition.

Albert Speer and Hitler (r.) on a winter walk on Obersalzberg

13
SS Guardhouse II

→ Hintereck, Map C2 The first checkpoint for visitors to the Obersalzberg was the ▷ SS Guardhouse I at Schießstättbrücke. At the access route to the innermost security area around the restricted zone ("Führersperrgebiet") marked "keep-off-grounds, Führer only" stood the main guardhouse of the "Leibstandarte SS Adolf Hitler" right by the ▷ "Berghof". In front of the gates, hundreds of curious spectators sometimes gathered to get a single glimpse of Hitler. Today only the stone foundation of the building remains on the mountain slope.

14
Model House, Film Archive and Kindergarten

⌂ Roderich Fick, 1941 → Hintereck, Map C2 Between the ▷ SS Barracks and the ▷ "Berghof" were three functional buildings. The biggest house served as a kindergarten for all Nazi-friendly inhabitants of Obersalzberg.
The model house held architectural models, which were presented to Hitler on the ▷ "Berghof". Together with his architect Albert Speer, he had planned numerous monumental axes and buildings in dozens of cities. The main focus was on Berlin, which was to be reconstructed over wide areas into "Germania", the world capital it was to become in 1950 after the "Final Victory".
The film archive stored news reports and movies which were shown on the ▷ "Berghof", in the ▷ SS Barracks, and in the ▷ Theatre Hall. Propaganda Minister Joseph Goebbels mostly made the selection personally. As Hitler's house manager Döhring reported, the "Führer" viewed the epic of the "Gone with the Wind" several times and Mickey Mouse and Charlie Chaplin movies. At the same time, the movie producer and actor Chaplin was busy viewing news reports about Hitler to prepare for his film "The Great Dictator". Chaplin's interview with the press in 1940 stirred up a veritable scandal. According to Chaplin, the premiere of the Hitler parody was to take place, of all places, in Berlin. After it

was released, Goebbels too got hold of a copy. The movie was rented out to the Reich Chancellery twice. It is reasonable to assume that Hitler himself also viewed it. According to the New York Times, the film is **"the most important movie ever made".**

15
Residential House of Martin Bormann

⌂ Roderich Fick, 1937 → Hintereck, Map C2 Next to his "boss" Hitler, Martin Bormann was the most influential person on the Obersalzberg. So that he and his family could always stay close to the "Führer", he confiscated the house of the paediatrician Dr. Richard Seitz. From here, Bormann was able to overview the ▷ Hotel "Zum Türken", the ▷ "Berghof" and wide parts of the remaining Obersalzberg. Acquisition and modernization of the building were paid out of the Nazi Party funds, as was the luxurious interior design. Through the basement, the residence was connected to the ▷ Shelter System of the Obersalzberg. While food was rationed in Germany, Bormann stored food here for decades. The British air raid in April 1945 destroyed the building completely.

14 Heil Hynkel! Charlie Chaplin as Adenoid Hynkel, dictator of Tomania in "The Great Dictator", 1940

16
Residential House of Hermann Göring

🏠 Alois Degano, 1933 → Hintereck, Map C2 The Eckerbichl was in its time the most elevated point on the Obersalzberg. From 1933 it had on its top a stone monument with the inscription **"Reich Chancellor Adolf Hitler Hill, 21 March 1933"**, on top of it a citation by the lyricist Ludwig Ganghofer: **"He who God loves, he drops off in the Berchtesgaden countryside."**

Shortly after that, the elevation was to be called exclusively "Göring Hill". On 17 August 1933, the Minister of the Reich Aviation Department came for a viewing of the property on the Eckerbichl. The 1,000 square metre area juxtaposed to the hill was given as a gift to the mighty Nazi administrator by the obsequious government of Bavaria.

As one of the few selected who were permitted to live on Hitler's mountain, he had a country house built here in alpine style, which was rather modest compared to his typical standards.

A few years later, Göring possessed larger private residences such as the feudal forest manor house "Carinhall" near Berlin or the "Reich Hunting Lodge" in East Prussia.

His country house on the Obersalzberg was expanded in 1941 by an annex and an open-air swimming pool. Additionally, the house now had underground shelter facilities at its disposal which, however, were not connected to Martin Bormann's major ▷ **Shelter System.**

30 metres underground, the "Führer Air Communication Central" (FFMZ – Führer-Flugmeldezentrale), a super-modern centre for aerial positioning, was carved into the rock. A big glass screen showed the air space over the Obersalzberg and allowed the coordination of the flak defense around the area. The underground rooms are preserved until today.

By contrast, Hermann Göring's country house was destroyed right down to the foundations during the British air raid on 25 April 1945.

Today, the "InterContinental Resort Berchtesgaden" built by the architect Herbert Kochta stands next door on the Eckerbichl. The construction of the 5-star luxury hotel in one of the most historically significant locations in Europe drew

16 Model of the "Resort" Hotel on the Eckerbichl

18 Entrance driveways into the former Coke Shelter, 2005

16 Göring during curling in front of his house, 1935

20 Residential Area Klaushöhe

much attention. The hotel management, however, confirmed that it would treat the past of the region with responsibility.

17
Greenhouse

→ Hintereck, Map C2 The Greenhouse measured 110 by 26 metres and was built underneath "Göring Hill" as part of Bormann's ▷ **Estate.** Above all, it provided the vegetarian Hitler with fruit and vegetables and also yielded fresh flowers for the ▷ **"Berghof".**

Only a few metres away from the high alpine Greenhouse originally stood the chapel "Maria Hilf", which had been the only church on the Obersalzberg. After Hitler had become Reich Chancellor no quiet masses were possible any more in the chapel 50 metres away from the ▷ **"Berghof".** Thousands of pilgrims came during the summer months and chanted: **"We want to see our Führer."** Shortly later, the whole property of the NSDAP on the Obersalzberg was fenced in.

The "Maria Hilf" chapel now stood in the middle of this off-limits area and was, if at all, reachable with only special identification. The catholic priest Johannes Baumann read the last mass on 18 January 1937. Not long afterwards, Bormann ordered the vacation of the chapel and had it torn down.

18
Coke Shelter

⌂ 1940 → Salzbergstraße, Hintereck, Map D2 Like a monolith, the coke shelter, measuring 38 by 28 metres and a height of 14 metres, reached into the treetops. It was built in six months in 1940 by Italian seasonal workers, was made of concrete covered with stone and had a capacity for 1,500 tons of coke. When Bormann came to inspect the completion, he had the whole façade torn down again, because the stones of the cover did not fit smoothly enough into each other. It took one year, finally, until completion and was a drastic example of the unscrupulous way in which Bormann used to waste money in the region. The coke shelter, costing 770,000 Reichsmark, is preserved to this day.

Eva Braun 1912–1945

Hitler met the 17-year old Eva Braun at the studio of his personal photographer Heinrich Hoffmann in Munich in 1929. The daughter of the vocational teacher Fritz Braun worked there as an assistant. The uncomplicated, young blond girl fitted into Hitler's view of women. **"There is nothing more beautiful than a young thing to educate for oneself. A girl of 18, 20 years, who is as pliable as wax."**

In 1936, Hitler took his "Tschapperl", as he called Eva, to the ▷ **"Berghof".** Officially, she was the private secretary of the "Führer", with only Hitler's cronies knowing that she was his secret lover. She adapted to the role of the hidden partner who was not to be seen when dignitaries visited. Her world on the Obersalzberg was an artificial idyll, which stood in stark contrast to the real world. While Hitler covered the whole of Europe with war and genocide, Eva Braun tackled her boredom with amateur movie making, with swimming excursions to the Königssee, and shopping trips to Florence. Despite the evidently pending defeat, she moved into the "Führerbunker" in Berlin on 7 March 1945. There she married Hitler on 29 April 1945. During the last hours of her life she proudly had others address her as "Mrs. Hitler". On 30 April 1945 the couple committed suicide together.

Transversal Cut through the Obersalzberg

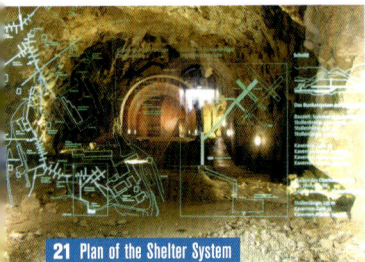
21 Plan of the Shelter System

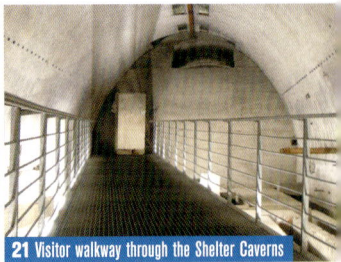
21 Visitor walkway through the Shelter Caverns

19
Roßfeld-Höhenringstraße
⌂ Fritz Todt, Head Construction Office Munich. 1938 → Roßfeldstraße, Map D 3

In 1927 the construction of the German Alpenstraße began, connecting Lake Constance with the Königssee. According to Bormann's planning, it was to go around the Berchtesgaden valley. The traversing of the Alps right over the hump of the Roßfeld was planned as a "demonstration of German road and engineer construction expertise". The project cost some 14 million Reichsmark. By the end of the war, works had progressed to the point of leaving just one uncompleted stretch of 800 metres, which was finished in 1953. For the defense of the Berchtesgaden air space, the SS installed numerous flak positions from 1943 on.

Today, Roßfeldstraße is a private toll road. In good weather conditions, it offers rewarding views of the Obersalzberg and the neighbouring Austrian Alps.

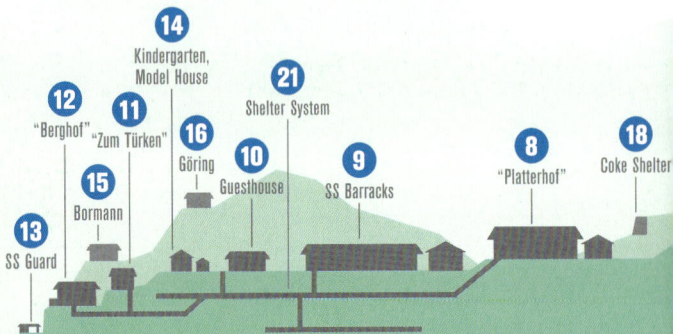

Roßfeld 1,600 metres

14 Kindergarten, Model House

12 "Berghof"
11 "Zum Türken"
21 Shelter System
16 Göring
15 Bormann
10 Guesthouse
9 SS Barracks
8 "Platterhof"
18 Coke Shelter
13 SS Guard

21
Shelter System
⌂ SS Army Geologist Battalion, 1945 → Obersalzberg, Map C 2

Upon Bormann's orders, the last major construction project was undertaken on the Obersalzberg in August 1943. The war, which was taking an increasingly unfavourable course from the Nazi perspective, prompted them to think more intensively about taking measures for protection against a variety of possible attacks. They started with a large labyrinth of underground shelters, which resulted in a 30 metres deep into the rock and a 4,6-kilometre-long tunnel system distributed over several storeys by the end of the war. The SS Army Geologist Battalion was responsible for this project. Up to 6,000 men were at their disposal, mostly Italian and Czech workers. "Reichsführer SS" Heinrich Himmler said: **It is a joyful duty of honour for us SS men to be allowed to build the air raid shelters on the Obersalzberg.**

20
Residential Area Klaushöhe

⌂ Roderich Fick, 1941 → Klaushöhe
1–19, Map E2 The Residential Area
Klaushöhe was home to the administrative employees of the Obersalzberg as
well as the families of the SS guards.
For the construction of these generous
houses, Bormann ordered only the most
precious materials including marble,
steel, copper, noblest woods and costly
plumbing, despite the scarcity of materials due to the war economy. Like all
other projects on the Obersalzberg,
these buildings, on which up to
4,000 workers laboured, were called
"Führer constructions". This gave
them the highest priority, and
they were built quickly and
without regard for costs.
Parts of this Residential
Area and the underground bomb shelter
facilities are still
preserved today.

1,837 metres: "Kehlsteinhaus"

Höher über NN 1,837 metres
24
"Kehlsteinhaus"

23
Kehlsteinstraße:
Bus Parking Place

Klaushöhe and **Buchen-
höhe** and under the
▷ **Estate.** For the about
1,000 workers of the ▷ **Shelter
Camp Antenberg,** raw shelter tunnels into
bare rock and bare caverns had to give
shelter in the event of air raid alarms.
Entrances to the shelters were protected
by steel doors. Narrow shooting embrasures mounted with machine guns were
installed behind them in perpendicular
walls. These walls were also expected
to protect against pressure waves from
bomb detonations. At the end of 1944
Bormann ordered the construction of
an even more secure Shelter System.
It was to be built at a depth of at least
100 metres into the mountain. The fortress was to shelter several 1,000 persons,
their provisions, weapons and vehicles.
Only a few short and uncompleted stretches were built by the end of the war.

As Hitler's coming to the Obersalzberg
for Christmas 1943 got known, highest
pressure was built up to finish for his
coming the first 130 metres shelter
facilities including Barracks underneath
the ▷ **"Berghof".** After eight weeks,
under greatest duress and sacrifices
for the workers, the goal was reached.
The rooms for Hitler and Eva Braun were
completely furnished. Parquet floors,
wooden paneling, air conditioning, built-in
radios, telephone lines, as well as tile-
covered kitchen and bathrooms stood
ready to use. Hitler's shelter facilities
encompassed 745 square metres; the
project was advanced up to beneath
the ▷ **SS Barracks** and the ▷ **Hotel
"Platterhof".** Through a hallway Bormann's
underground Reich was within reach.
Added were shelter tunnels under the
"Göring House", the ▷ **Residential Areas**

21 Shelter entrance to the Hintereckstollen

The Shelter System

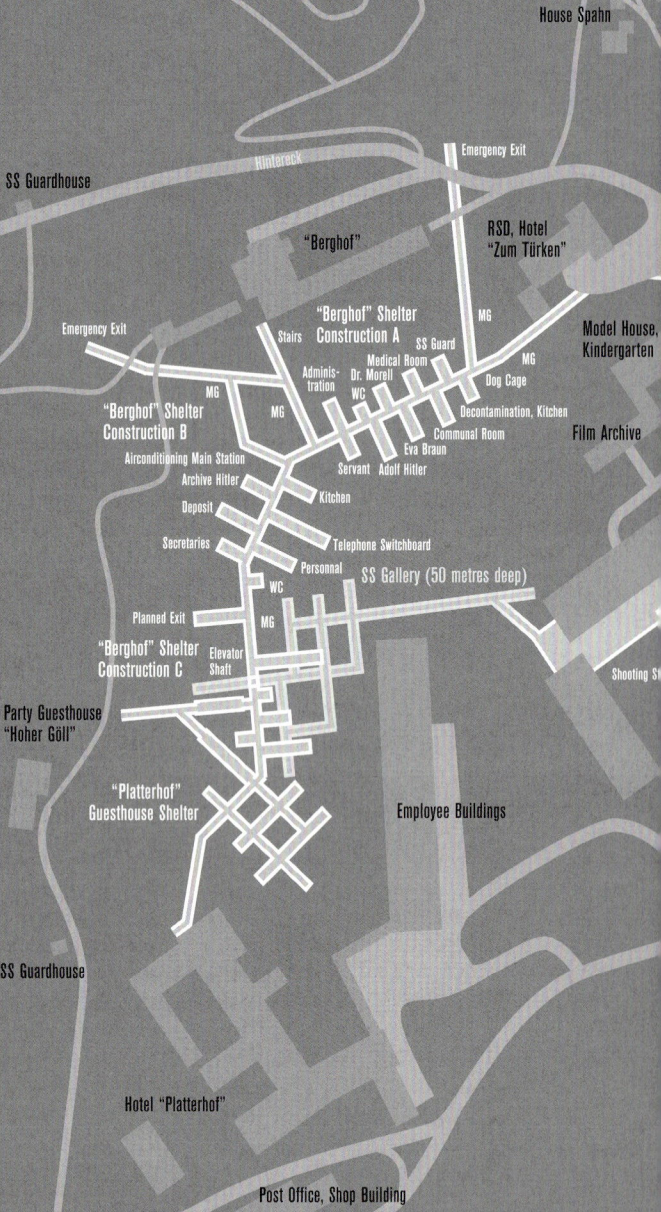

House Spahn

Emergency Exit

SS Guardhouse

Hintereck

"Berghof"

RSD, Hotel
"Zum Türken"

Emergency Exit

"Berghof" Shelter
Construction A

Stairs

SS Guard

MG

Model House,
Kindergarten

Administration

Medical Room
Dr. Morell

WC

MG

Dog Cage

MG

"Berghof" Shelter
Construction B

MG

Decontamination, Kitchen

Film Archive

Communal Room

Airconditioning Main Station

Eva Braun

Archive Hitler

Servant   Adolf Hitler

Deposit

Kitchen

Secretaries

Telephone Switchboard

Personal

SS Gallery (50 metres deep)

WC

Planned Exit

MG

"Berghof" Shelter
Construction C

Elevator
Shaft

Shooting St

Party Guesthouse
"Hoher Göll"

"Platterhof"
Guesthouse Shelter

Employee Buildings

SS Guardhouse

Hotel "Platterhof"

Post Office, Shop Building

21 Shelter gallery

21 Living quarters

21 Storage room

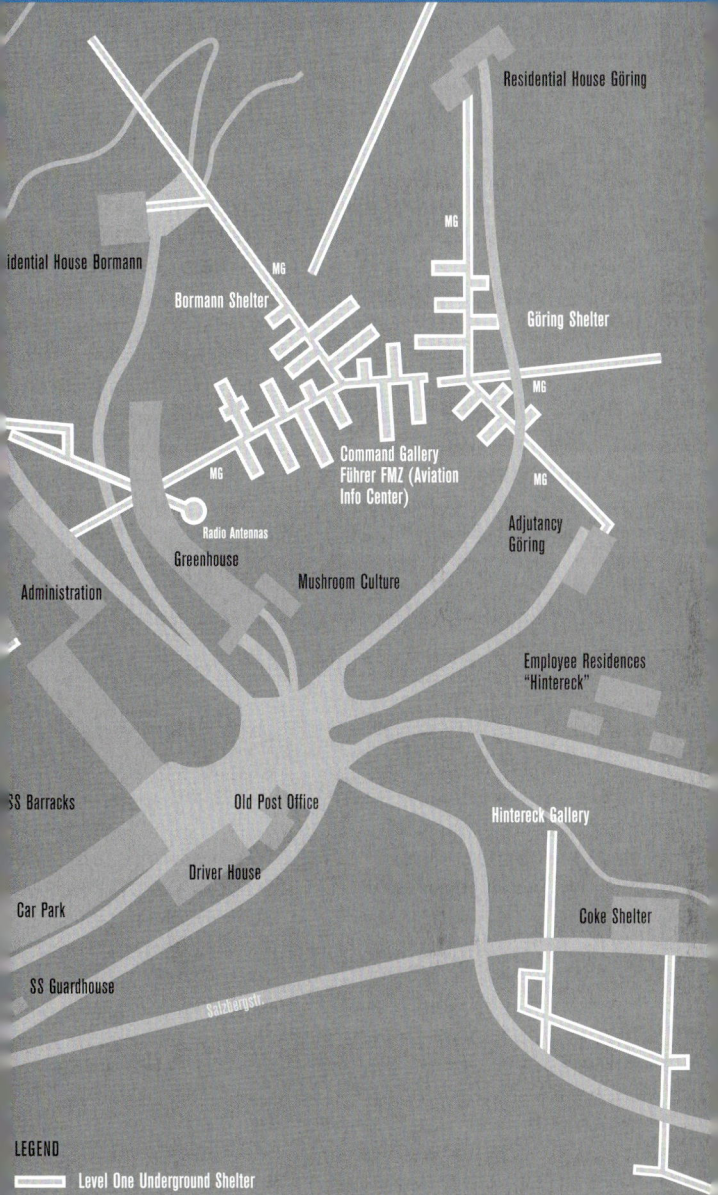

Residential House Göring

idential House Bormann

MG

Bormann Shelter

MG

Göring Shelter

MG

Command Gallery
Führer FMZ (Aviation
Info Center)

MG

MG

Adjutancy
Göring

Radio Antennas

Greenhouse

Mushroom Culture

Administration

Employee Residences
"Hintereck"

SS Barracks

Old Post Office

Hintereck Gallery

Driver House

Car Park

Coke Shelter

SS Guardhouse

Salzbergstr.

LEGEND

Level One Underground Shelter

Level Two Underground SS Shelter

Aboveground Buildings

Streets and Walkways

21 Shaft passage

21 Cavern

21 Metal closet

22
Residential Area Buchenhöhe

⌂ Hermann Giesler, 1942 → Buchen-höhe 1–84, Map F2 While war raged in German cities and bombs fell, new con-structions were started on the Obersalz-berg regardless. The Residential Area Buchenhöhe was erected in 1942, based on plans by the Munich architect Hermann Giesler. Similarly to the ▷ **Residential Area Klaushöhe,** the houses were sub-sumed under the "war priority" construc-tion program.

Financing came from the "Adolf Hitler Donation" funded annually by German industry since 1933 for Hitler's direct discretionary spending (total contributions amounted to 800 million Reichsmark by 1945). The grounds for construction work were understandably difficult in this unyielding terrain. Forest areas had to be cut down, mountain rivers detoured, metre-deep foundations deto-nated into the rock and precipices had to be bridged.

Within the shortest time, 40 private hou-ses stood. Garages, a shopping facility, a kindergarten, an open-air swimming pool, a sports hall, and a fire station were added. The long-distance heating facility alone cost one million Reichsmark. The British bombing raid of 25 April 1945 destroyed some of the buildings. Parts of the Residential Area are used today by an asthma clinic.

23
Kehlsteinstraße

⌂ Fritz Todt, Firma Leonhard Moll, 1938 → Kehlsteinstraße. Map C4, E4 After Hitler had consented to Bormann's plans to build a Teahouse and Guesthouse on the 1,837-metre-high Kehlstein in

1936, construction works began in the spring of 1937. The 6.5-kilometre-long mountain road with a difference in altitude of 700 metres was built from Obersalzberg up to shortly beneath the Kehlstein moun-tain top, ending there on a small plateau.

22 Residential Area Buchenhöhe

23 Kehlsteinstraße

At times, up to 3,500 workers were attributed to this stretch and housed in simple barrack camps directly on the mountain slope. The highest stood at 1,640 metres, only 200 metres below the mountain-top. Construction materials and machines had to be transported to the individual plateaus with construction sites by means of carrier columns and a cable railway. Numerous detonations, artificial earth mounds, five tunnels, and elaborate bridge constructions with only one turn-ing point were necessary for overcoming natural obstacles.

Due to continued postponement of dead-lines by Bormann, an inconceivable pres-sure of time weighed on the project, which was pressed forward during the whole of 1937. Even during winter, the workers had to continue their dangerous labour in the face of ice, snow and ava-lanche risk. Until its completion in the summer of 1938, several fatal accidents had occurred.

Construction costs for the total project Kehlstein, which was not accessible to the public at all, amounted to a gigantic sum of 30 million Reichsmark (by current standards approximately 375 million Euro).

Since the closure of Kehlsteinstraße for private traffic in 1952, special public buses take visitors from the Obersalzberg to the car park directly below the ▷ **"Kehlsteinhaus".** The last 131 metres altitude can then be taken at a leisurely pace by lift or on foot.

Obersalzberg Visitors

The first visitors to the ▷ **"Berghof"** were Hitler's cronies such as Goebbels, Göring and Himmler. The foreign visitors whom yet well known, came to visit the Obersalzberg to present Hitler with two prototypes of the VW Käfer. Hitler had com-

Reception of Bulgaria's King Boris, 1943

Hitler and Himmler (back) in VW bug, 1944

Hitler received by the end of the 30s on the Obersalzberg were to suggest to the German public that the "Führer" was an internationally reputed head of government concerned with peace. Visitors who were particularly profiled were the former British prime minister David Lloyd George, who had co-signed the Versailles Treaty in 1919, the abdicated King Edward VIII, or the acting prime minister Arthur Neville Chamberlain, who visited the ▷ **"Berghof"** on 15 September 1938. During the preliminary talks on the "Munich Agreement", he negotiated with Hitler over a solution to the conflict Hitler had provoked between Germany and Czechoslovakia. It was to remain one of the rare visits of important active foreign politicians on the ▷ **"Berghof"**.
As early as 11 July 1936 an engineer by the name of Ferdinand Porsche, then not

missioned him with its design in 1933. In 1934 Hitler sketched his updated desires for changes on a napkin. With over 21 million cars, the Käfer, built until 2003, was to become the biggest-selling automobile in history.

During the Second World War, Hitler received mostly heads of state of vassal states at his upper Bavarian refuge, including Italy's dictator Mussolini and his foreign minister Count Ciano, or King Boris III of Bulgaria.
In Hitler's absence, by contrast, Eva Braun invited her relatives, friends and prominent guests from the worlds of art, sports and film. Among them were the national sculptor Josef Thorak, the boxer Max Schmeling, various UFA starlets and members of the Munich Gärtnerplatztheater.

Hitler and Mussolini on the "Berghof", 20 January 1941

24 Door knob Kehlstein shelter gallery

24 Flak platforms at "Kehlsteinhaus"

24 West side of the "Kehlsteinhaus"

24 "Kehlsteinhaus" with view of the German Alps

24 Sun terrace

24 124-metre-long tunnel to brass lift

The "Kehlsteinhaus"

24
"Kehlsteinhaus"

⌂ Roderich Fick 1939 → Kehlstein, Map F4 ⏱ May–October The "Kehlsteinhaus" was conceived in 1936 by the Munich architect Roderich Fick. It was commissioned by Bormann as a representative Teahouse and Guesthouse. The NSDAP intended to offer the "Kehlsteinhaus" as a gift to Hitler for his 50th birthday in 1939.

As the ▷ **Kehlsteinstraße** could not be built up to the narrow top of the mountain, an alternative was chosen to the already cost-intensive project. Money was not an issue, as was known for any of the projects on the Obersalzberg. Initially, workers built a 126-metre-long tunnel horizontally into the solid rock, starting out at the little parking lot below the "Kehlsteinhaus". From the end of the tunnel, a 131-metre-high vertical tunnel was blown into the natural rock up to the "Kehlsteinhaus" on the mountain top. The difference in altitude has been overcome since 1939 with a lift built by the Berlin company Carl Flohr. The lift had a mirror-like metal sheeted spacious interior.

Compared to the immense construction costs of around 30 million Reichsmark, the "Kehlsteinhaus" had extremely little practical value. At a height of 1,834 metres it was meant to give important foreign dignitaries an unforgettable view over the surrounding landscape. Because Hitler could not cope with the thin air at this altitude, he was constantly plagued by headaches, which meant he rarely came here. Frequent guests however were Eva Braun and Martin Bormann.

The heart of the building was the octagonal socializing hall (Gesellschaftshalle). It was constructed in a rustic alpine style with ceiling beams, granite walls, marble floor and a red open fireplace – a gift of the Italian dictator, "Il Duce" Benito Mussolini. Over the fireplace hung a gift of the Japanese emperor, a valuable wall tapestry.

Juxtaposed to this were a few functional rooms such as the kitchen and the quarters for SS guards, an office that Hitler never used and the Scharitz-Stube.

In good weather conditions, the windproof sun terrace still offers a pretty view of the Königssee and the Berchtesgaden area.

For the security of the dictator and his guests, the whole area around the "Kehlsteinhaus" was enclosed by a 10-kilometre barbed-wire fence, patrolled by Mountain Infantrymen (SS-Gebirgsjäger). In 1944 four flak installations were added, positioned on concrete platforms around the "Kehlsteinhaus" to protect against allied bombing raids. These flak installations are still visible today.

US intelligence suspected that deep under the mountain, the military facilities of Hitler's ▷ **Alpine Fortress** were possibly hidden.

During post-war times the newly named "Eagle's Nest" was reserved for US soldiers, the metal-plated lift even only for officers, while lower ranks had to make the way on foot. High-ranking guests included the US generals Dwight D. Eisenhower and Omar Bradley. Prior to detonation by the Allies in 1951, the "Kehlsteinhaus" was under the auspices of the Berchtesgaden district administrator Theodor Jacob.

Today the building is the property of the Berchtesgaden Foundation, which also runs the ▷ **Obersalzberg Documentation Centre.** It is one of the most frequently visited sites in the region.

Kiel

Bremen   Hamburg

WESTPHALIAN PLAIN

Münster

Paderborn   Hannover

Brunswick

THE RUHR   Berlin

Remagen   Magdeburg

Fra

Kassel   Gu

Cott

Frankfurt   Erfurt   Leipzig

Dresden

Würzburg

Karlsruhe   BOHEMIA

Nürnberg   Prag

Stuttgart   Pilsen   BAS

HITLER'S INNER FORTRESS?

Augsburg

Munich   Danube R.

Innsbruck   Linz

Berchtesgaden   Vienna

Brenner Pass   Bolzano   AUSTRIAN ALPS

Graz

Verona

Trieste

2n
Ukr

& Br 8th

The Alpine Fortress

In the autumn of 1944 the Second World War was as good as lost for the German army. Not so for the fanatic Waffen SS. Heinrich Himmler had the megalomaniacal plan to change the destiny of the "Thousand Year Reich" with his and his paladins' continued fighting from the Alpine Fortress. The US troops were prepared for a bloody final battle in the Salzburg region, but the "bulwark in the Alps" finally remained only wishful thinking on the part of the Nazis.

In the summer of 1943, Hitler transferred the command over the protection of Obersalzberg from allied air raids to a flak and fog division of the SS. They positioned numerous flaks and fog-producing machines at strategically important points of mountain-tops and high plateaus all around Obersalzberg and in the region of Berchtesgaden. The "Central Aviation Alarm Unit of the Führer" (Führer-Flugmeldezentrale) in a 30-metre-deep shelter under the "Göring Hill" coordinated the defense and set off air raid alarms at the approach of enemy planes. The SS fog division had the mission to hide Obersalzberg under a dense cloud of chemically produced fog around the clock.

In the spring of 1945 Hitler's ▷ **"Berghof"** was painted dark and camouflaged with nets. The "Führer" himself was long gone from his vacation domicile, having left for Berlin on 14 July 1944, not knowing that he was never to return. Construction work on the underground ▷ **Shelter System** of Obersalzberg was feverishly continued nonetheless under Martin Bormann's orders. He still hoped that he could move out of the way with the "Führer" to the Alpine Fortress before the Red Army surrounded Berlin. But Hitler had decided to stay in Berlin.

The last high-ranking Nazi inhabitant of the mountain idyll was Marshal of the Reich Hermann Göring, from 21 April 1945 on. A few days later he had his country seat Carinhall near Berlin blown up. On 20 April he had presented Hitler with the obligatory congratulations for his 56th birthday. Immediately afterwards he removed himself into the idyll of the upper Bavarian mountain landscape, which was still untouched by the war. With him, numerous wagonloads of treasures stolen from the art world throughout Europe arrived in Berchtesgarden. Göring, officially Hitler's successor since 1933, wired a request to Berlin on 23 April 1945, asking whether the threat of a pending victory over Berlin by the Soviet Army warranted that he now take over the total leadership of the Reich. Enraged at this enquiry, which was portrayed by Bormann as betrayal, Hitler immediately suspended Göring's official functions and ordered his arrest. The SS put Göring under arrest in his luxurious country seat on 24 April 1945.

As early as 1941, the Allies had produced photographs of the individual buildings with long distance reconnaissance planes. The US Ministry of War used these pictures to construct a target information sheet of the area and left it under British Bomber Command.

British anti-Hitler postage stamp, which was brought into circulation in the German Reich ("Lost Empire")

Bombing Target Obersalzberg

The Allies called the ▷ **"Kehlsteinhaus"** the "Eagle's Nest". It was Target A on their list. They suspected gigantic shelter facilities deep inside the mountain as a substantial part of the Alpine Fortress. Target B was Hitler's ▷ **"Berghof",** which received the name "Rock of the Guard" ("Wachenfels" [sic]).

Bombing raid alerts were nothing new on the Obersalzberg since the beginning of 1945. However, enemy planes had only flown over the Berchtesgaden region. On 25 April this was to change. Without forewarning, suddenly the first British Lancaster bombers appeared over Kehl-stein at 09:00 am. The air raid alarm came too late, the fog divisions had failed, and the first bombing wave inca-pacitated the flak positions. Altogether 300 airplanes had participated in the raid and, besides six casualties within their own ranks, had reduced nearly the whole Obersalzberg to rubble with 1,800 tons of fire and detonation bombs.

The underground ▷ **Shelter System** with-stood even the 12,000 pounds of British bombs. About 3,500 people survived underground, leaving only six dead and several wounded. Göring, who was under

Residential House Göring

Residential House Bormann

Greenhouse

Kindergarten

Hotel "Zum Türken"

"Berghof"

Shelter Emergency Exit

SS Guardhouse

arrest, had survived in his shelter and was the only party official to visit the destruction in person.

The ▷ **"Berghof"** had received heavy hits, the ▷ Hotel **"Zum Türken"** and the ▷ Hotel **"Platterhof"** were slightly damaged. Bormann's and Göring's homes and the SS Barracks were destroyed, Speer's houses by contrast remained unscathed.

During the last days of April 1945 chaos and anarchy prevailed in the "Führer region off-limits" ("Führersperrgebiet"). Looting removed all the stores from the ruins and shelters: food, cigarettes, clothes, furniture, art objects.

In the "Führerbunker" in Berlin, Hitler showed no reaction when he received

First rest for GIs on the "Berghof"

the news of Obersalzberg's destruction. He had already essentially given up on his life.

In the afternoon of 4 May 1945 the first US troops of the 101st infantry division reached Berchtesgaden. The regional official Theodor Jacob came towards them with a white flag, surrendering the area without fighting. The first allied soldiers

To "Kehlsteinhaus"

Residential Area Klaushöhe

Kehlsteinstraße

SS Barracks

Salzbergstraße

"Platterhof"

Shelter Entry

Party Guesthouse

Ruined landscape of Obersalzberg after the British bombing raid, photograph May 1945 who reached the Obersalzberg were two French officers. They saw the tail lights of the SS Mountain Infantry disappearing just as, at that very moment, the roof of the ▷ "Berghof" burst into flames. In the basement, among countless wine and champagne bottles, they found a large Dutch flag. Without ado, they transformed it into a French Tricolore and hung it from the porch as a symbol of victory. The shelters were still filled with riches and precious items and were thoroughly plundered by the victors and local villagers.

At the same time, the Americans caught numerous Nazi functionaries and prominent people in their net who had made Upper Bavaria and the Alpine Fortress their last escape resort. For example, they caught Leni Riefenstahl. Writer Erich Kästner, who had fled from Berlin to Austria with an UFA film team, commented in his diary about those arrests: **"Julius Streicher was caught in Berchtesgaden. Himmler committed suicide with cyanide under British arrest. When he was caught he had shaved his moustache and wore a black patch over one eye. Robert Ley grew a beard. It is like a mask hire shop. There are no limits to indignity. The catastrophe ends as joke and as show business. The face of the master race with a false moustache!"**

Last Bastion Alpine Fortress

"Reichsführer SS" Heinrich Himmler, who had been arrested shortly before, had already toyed with the idea of erecting a "Bulwark of resistance" in the Alps in 1944. Hitler too had kept this option open as long as possible in the face of the threat of defeat. His hope was that the "unnatural" coalition between the USA and the Soviet Union would break apart. In that case he could have made a separate peace treaty with the Western Allies in order to then jointly fight the main enemy, the communist Soviet Union. In April 1945 as the final battle for Berlin began, large parts of the commands, offices, and provisions institutions of the German armed forces and the Waffen SS had already been transferred to the Alpine Fortress. SS Standartenführer and "Mussolini's rescuer" Otto Skorzeny was to form the "Alpenland" corps here from the remainder of his divisions. In the immediate vicinity, among the mountains and lakes of the Salzkammergut and above all in Ausseerland, several other mass murderers of the "Third Reich" had also sought refuge: Ernst Kaltenbrunner, Chief of the Reich Central Security Office, Heinrich Müller, Chief of the Gestapo, and SS-Obersturmbannführer Adolf Eichmann, director of the "Jewish Evacuation Department". His signature had sent millions of people to the death

US soldiers in the huge, destroyed 9 by 3.60 metre panorama window of the "Berghof", May 1945

> ## "The news that Adolf Hitler is dead seemed at first incomprehensible. We had hoped too much for his arrival in the fictitious Alpine Fortress."
> (Otto Skorzeny, SS-Standartenführer)

camps. Now the Nazis wanted to organize the last "defense battle" from here. Reportedly, Eichmann was accompanied by 22 crates filled, among other things, with gold teeth and wedding rings from the concentration camps, worth eight million dollars. Kaltenbrunner too figured on an SS list for moving heavy loads of precious stones, gold bars and coins from the stocks of the German Reichsbank to the Ausseerland. Additionally, Kaltenbrunner had a forgery, constructed in the Sachsenhausen concentration camp, transferred to the upper Austrian external camp Ebensee at the beginning of 1945, to continue mass production of British pound notes, US dollars and documents. Ebensee was equally a center for the planned underground arms production of "miracle weapons" such as the "V2 rocket". In gigantic mines, thousands of concentration camp prisoners were to produce tanks, small fire arms, ammunition and gasoline. Factories such as the "Seegrotte" in Hinterbrühl had already begun the serial production of new kinds of jet planes.

The intention to "free" Germany from here after waiting out the right moment in the imaginary Alpine Fortress failed. After the southern front had capitulated on 2 May 1945 in the hands of SS Obergruppenführer Karl Wolff, Himmler's employee for many years, US troops took the "bulwark", which was presumed to be armed to the teeth, with great ease.

Counterfeit pound note on Kaltenbrunner's orders

Many Nazi war criminals managed to escape to South America, as did Eichmann. Others, like the torture expert Klaus Barbie, were taken over by US intelligence.

On 30 April 1952, the 7th anniversary of Hitler's death, the charred ruin of the "Bernhof" was detonated

BERCHTESGADEN The upper Bavarian spa town was extended into a second seat of government after Hitler came to power. To this aim an external arm of the Berlin Reich Chancellery was built in the Stanggaß district. Representative new buildings gave the place a new face, including the Main Railway Station for the reception of foreign dignitaries and an accordingly grand hotel for appropriate accommodation of guests. Additionally, the region became an important military location for stationing the new Barracks for the Mountain Infantry (Gebirgsjäger).

1
Main Railway Station
⌂ Ernst Stroebel, 1940 → Bahnhofplatz 1, Map E3 In the 1920s, the community had already started to apply to the railway administration of the Reich for a new station building. After Hitler had "seized" power at the beginning of 1933, Berchtesgaden's transportation and tourism flourished enormously. Thousands of tourists travelled to Obersalzberg during the summer months to get a glimpse of the "Führer". Hitler had selected the ▷ **"Berghof"** for his second government seat. This made it necessary to erect representative buildings. The new railway station, which was totally oversized for the small community, was reserved for passenger transportation. Industrial transportation was to operate through the new station "Berchtesgaden North". Together with the neighbouring ▷ **Post Office,** the Main Railway Station was to function as the gateway to the "German Alpine Route" in Berchtesgaden. Further plans dating from 1938 provided for an extension of the station, continuing two tracks to Salzburg. The last relict of these unachieved construction plans is a 250-metre-long tunnel under the city centre. During Hitler's presence in Obersalzberg, his "Special Führer Train" stood here, protected from Allied air raids.

Toward the end of the war, Hermann Göring stationed wagons here with the most part of his collection of his stolen art objects. The railway employees used a mine as an air raid shelter.

Even though the construction of the railway station was not ranked high on the list of war priorities, about 600 French forced labourers had to work on the project in 1944. The station, only slightly damaged during the war, belongs today to the German railway system (Deutsche Bahn AG).

2
Post Office
⌂ Franz Holzhammer, Hans Schnetzer, Walter Schmidt, 1937 → Bahnhofplatz 4, Map E3 A large post office was erected in connection with the construction of the new ▷ **Main Railway Station.** The construction amounted to 800,000 Reichsmark. A marble mosaic by the artist Max Lacher on the front wall of the post office still greets visitors coming from the west side along the Alpine route to Berchtesgaden. It shows the oversize depiction of a man leaning on a shield with the historical coat of arms of Berchtesgaden. His right hand holds a banner with the swastika flag. The swastika was rendered unrecognizable shortly after the American troops arrived.

14 Tourist poster by Ludwig Hohlwein, 1929 (Berchtesgaden – The pearl of the Bavarian Alps)

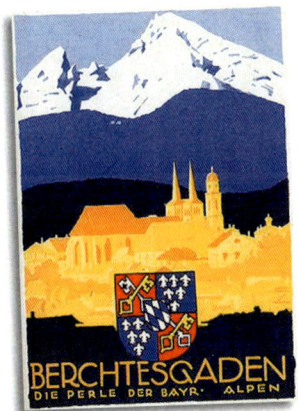

BERCHTESGADEN
DIE PERLE DER BAYR · ALPEN

TIMELINE BERCHTESGADEN HISTORY 1888–1960

1914 Beginning of World War I

1918 Bavarian king fled to St. Bartholomä

1927 Hitler rents House "Wachenfeld"

1933 Hitler bec[...] Reich Chancellor and acquires Ho[...] "Wachenfeld", fr[...] 1936 on "Bergho[...]

1888 First Railway from Bad Reichenhall to Berchtesgaden

1921 Plant Protection Zone Berchtesgaden becomes National Park

1923 Hitler first on Obersalzberg

Empire	Weimarer Republic	
	1918	1933

3
Area Forum

⌂ 1938 → Bahnhofplatz, Map E3

Berchtesgaden had advanced to an important centre of power of the "Third Reich" due to the new constructions for the NSDAP on Obersalzberg and the satellite office of the ▷ **Reich Chancellery** in Strub. The image of the city was therefore to be improved to live up to its new representative functions. Constructions to express the new concept included the ▷ **Main Railway Station**, the ▷ **Post Office**, and the ▷ **Hotel "Berchtesgadener Hof"**. In addition, the NSDAP Regional Head and Mayor Kammerer desired extensive transformations of the square in front of the Main Railway Station. The focus of these transformations was an Area Forum of the NSDAP, planned since 1935 as a representative reception gate for the various party buildings in the surroundings. According to Kammerer, the aim was to make **"Berchtesgaden into a gem of the Great German Reich".** Due to the war preparations the works were stopped in 1938 and the remains were removed in 1945.

4
Youth Hostel "Adolf Hitler"/ Youth Hostel "Berchtesgaden"

⌂ Georg Zimmermann, 1938
→ Struberberg 6, Strub, Map C3

"To give youth an opportunity to get to know that country in which the house of the Führer stands, the Youth Hostel 'Adolf Hitler' was built in Strub in 1935 by the local architect Georg Zimmermann", said the Nazi propaganda in 1939. The hostel counted among the prestige objects of the "Third Reich" youth policy. Based on the Berchtesgaden style of construction, raw materials exclusively from that region were used and finished by local artisans. After its completion, up to 400 young people were able to stay at the hostel in Strub with a view of Hitler's ▷ **"Kehlsteinhaus".** For National Socialism, Youth Hostels were an important instrument of preparation for later military service. **"Where the German country is most beautiful, where Germans work the hardest, where German people are fighting at borders that is where German youth of all regions meets, that is where the Youth Hostels stand."**

1 Eagle sculpture with view over Berchtesgaden Valley, 2005

1939 Beginning of World War II

1941 "Operation Barbarossa", surprise attack on the Soviet Union

Dictator Mussolini visits Obersalzberg

938 British Premier Minister hamberlain visits Obersalzberg

25 April 1945 Bombing raid on Obersalzberg

4 May 1945 Allied troops arrive

23 May 1949 Foundation of the Federal Republic of Germany

1960 150 years' celebration of Berchtesgaden's incorporation into Bavaria

"Third Reich" | **Federal Republic of Germany**

1945

The building complex survived the war undamaged and is still used as a Youth Hostel today.

5
BDM Reich Sports School / Senior Citizen's Home "Insula"

⌂ Carl Vessar, 1938 → Insulaweg 1, Map A3 "Youth should lead youth," was a maxim of the "Hitler Youth" (HJ – Hitler-Jugend). The "League of German Maidens" (BDM – Bund Deutscher Mädel) was part of this organization from 1930. Its aim was to educate girls to party conformism and respect for authority in the spirit of the Nazi ideology. BDM membership was compulsory for all girls and young women between the ages of 10 and 21 from 1936 on. Its curriculum consisted of obedience, responsibility, discipline, readiness for sacrifice and self-control of the body. Courses on worldviews taught the "science of race", folk music, dance, domestic skills and sports.

As the Germans were to be integrated at an early age into the Nazi system by these principles, the construction of BDM and HJ hostels became a priority. In Berchtesgaden, a BDM Reich sports school was under construction since 1938, but remained uncompleted by the end of the war.

Shortly after US troops had entered the region in May 1945, the 36th US infantry division established a camp for German prisoners of war (POW) in the Berchtesgaden BDM school. Among the most prominent prisoners was the infamous "Governor General" of occupied Poland, Hans Frank. He had come into US imprisonment on 4 May 1945, initially unrecognized. As an inmate of the Berchtesgaden POW camp, he slit his wrists on 6 May 1945. He eventually identified himself to the US medical staff who had saved his life. He voluntarily handed over his diaries, in which he had kept records of all the brutalities of his cruel reign in Poland. He had to stand trial as one of the main war criminals before the Nuremberg International Military Court and was executed on 16 October 1946.

After its dissolution, the prison camp served as a camp for "Displaced

1 Railway Station waiting hall

2 Wall mosaic

The Mountain Infantry

The Bavarian Mountain Infantry was founded as a special troop for the defence of the Alpine borders and offensive battles on Alpine grounds under extreme weather conditions. After Hitler came to power, a priority aim was the training of "elite soldiers" for the pending war of conquest. For this purpose, the troops received special uniforms, munitions, winter training on skis, as well as mule units. Towards the end of the war helicopters were added.

The Mountain Infantry fought in the Second World War from Norway's glacial waters to Italy and Greece, Crete and the most advanced front stretches deep into the Soviet Union. In the Caucasus a commando was sent ahead to climb the 5,633-metre-high Elbrus mountain and hoist the "Reich War Flag" for propaganda purposes.

Each year at Pentecost in Mittenwald, veterans and active soldiers meet to commemorate at the honorary monument to the German Mountain Infantry for those who died in the two World Wars. These commemorations are constantly accompanied by demonstrators recalling the war crimes of the German army and the Mountain Infantry divisions. In September 1943, in fact, units of the Mountain Infantry murdered 4,000 Italian prisoners of war on the Greek island of Kephallenia. Many further massacres and other crimes were committed in Italy, France, Finland, Yugoslavia and the Soviet Union.

Persons". Predominantly, former forced labourers and concentration camp inmates from Eastern Europe ended up here, who wandered in tens of thousands around Germany on their way home after their liberation.

Today the former buildings of the BDM Reich Sports School house the senior citizen's home "Insula". The former BDM sports hall serves as church and masses have been held in it for more than 50 years.

6
Mountain Infantry Barracks
⌂ Bruno Biehler, 1938 → In der Strub 3, Bischofswiesen Strub, Map B3

On 15 October 1935 the 100th Mountain Infantry regiment was founded. The army leadership selected Berchtesgaden for the garrison of Battalion II. Elaborate military quarters were established in the style of the Berchtesgaden farms. The monumental fortress-like tower construction as entrance contrasted with them. On 15 November 1938 the first recruits arrived. Exactly one year later, Battalion II was transferred to Slovakia. The Second World War had begun. During the war, the Berchtesgaden "Hunters" (Mountain Infantry Troops) were sent to war scenes throughout Europe.

From 1942 on, the military quarters also served Hitler's army leadership as vacation housing during the many holidays of the "Führer" in Obersalzberg. Added to that, during the last months of the war the newly founded General Leadership of the German Armed Forces, Division South, was also stationed here.

Since 1957 the Barracks have housed the 232nd Mountain Infantry Battalion of the German Bundeswehr. The almost 5-metre-high stone sculpture with an uprising lion on the square in front of the Barracks commemorates the Mountain Infantry men who lost their lives during the Second World War. An exhibition in the tower informs visitors about the history of this location.

4 Youth Hostel "Adolf Hitler", 1939

5 "League of German Maidens" in the Hitler Youth

6 Mountain Infantry on parade

6 Mountain Infantry in the Caucasus, 1942

6 Barracks of the Bundeswehr Mountain Infantry Battalion 232

The Reich Chancellery

7
Reich Chancellery, Berchtesgaden Office

Alois Degano, 1937 → Urbanweg 28, Stanggaß, Map B2 After Hitler was named Reich Chancellor, Obersalzberg reached increasing significance as a second government seat. The "Führer" spent five months per year on average on the ▷ **"Berghof"**. During these periods, therefore, a delegation of the Berlin Reich Chancellery had to be present as well. The Berlin administrators and secretaries were initially boarded in Berchtesgaden pensions. At the end of 1935, Hitler decided to have a regular office of the Reich Chancellery installed in Berchtesgaden. A property on the route to Bischofswiesen in Stanggaß was chosen for this office. The completion of this construction cost over 1–3 million Reichsmark (over 16 million euros by current standards).

On 17 January 1937, the building was inaugurated in the presence of Hitler and the Head of the Reich Chancellery, Hans Heinrich Lammers. In July 1937 the building was ready for use. In contrast to Albert Speer's monumental conception of the New Reich Chancellery in Berlin, this rather modest Berchtesgaden "service office" fit into the architectural style of the region. The whole area became a strongly guarded security zone, surrounded by accommodation for employees. Hitler's closest military counsels General Field Marshal Wilhelm Keitel, Chief of the Upper Military Command of the German Armed Forces, and Head of Generals Alfred Jodl, Chief of the Army Leadership, each had their own residence here. During the war the chancellery building was also used for the 50-strong team of the headquarters of the "Führer" in April and June 1942.

The fact that Hitler made all important decisions himself meant the Reich Chancellery was of secondary value. From 1938, no cabinet meetings took place. The ministers were degraded to chiefs of administration of their respective domains. They were mostly dependent on the Chief of the Reich Chancellery, Hans Heinrich Lammers, who completed Hitler's administrative work. Lammers remained unappreciated by the latter. It was Lammers who communicated all important information to the "Führer".

Hitler had an office in the satellite administration of the Reich Chancellery in Berchtesgaden but rarely used it. Head of Generals Alfred Jodl was "harder working". It was here that he completed the plans for **"Operation Barbarossa"**, the surprise attack on the Soviet Union. At the beginning of June 1941, he signed the **"Commissary Command"** Hitler had

7 Reich Chancellery, Berchtesgaden Office, 1937

requested, which ordered captured Soviet Politburo Commissaries to be shot on sight. This command for murder now definitely implicated the German Wehrmacht in the crimes of the Nazi dictatorship. Toward the end of the war, the Reich Chancellery also got its own air raid shelter. It gobbled up 700,000 Reichsmark (about 9 million euros). The total premises are 550 metres long and 40 metres deep into the ground. While Obersalzberg was reduced to rubble by the Allies, the satellite office in Stanggaß remained unscathed and was taken over by US troops. In May 1945, the 101st US Airborne Division under General Taylor occupied the building.

Until 1996, the premises served the Armed Forces Recreation Centre as headquarters, a vacation retreat for US soldiers. The interior designs of Nazi times were largely preserved in their original state. Until 1996, the keys on the switchboard of the historical telephone device with its connection pins carried still the designations of the time. Those read "Führer", "Adjutant to the Führer" or "Berghof". The telecabin "F 36" is now housed in the German Technology Museum in Berlin.

As a relic of the times of the former owners, the space above the portal still carries a Reich Eagle sculpted in red stone. The Swastika was removed from its claws. The building is now private property and is rented out.

7 Portal of the former Reich Chancellery, 2005

Alfred Jodl 1890–1946

Alfred Jodl was born in Würzburg on 10 May 1890. During the First World War he advanced to officer status. In 1923 he met Hitler. Shortly before the Second World War he was assigned Chief of the German Armed Forces Head Command.

As a "modern" general he realized the importance of the cooperation between the land, air and marine forces. His attack plan against Denmark and Norway is still part of the lecture materials of the West Point US Military Academy. After the victorious attack in the west he advanced to Hitler's closest military adviser. He contributed to all German military actions of the Second World War and remained a decisive voice until its end.

After the defeat near Moscow in December 1941, he reportedly no longer believed in German victory. He was a unique voice in contradicting Hitler and paid for it by falling into disgrace. **"It is insanity to still continue the war at this point"**, Alfred Jodl wrote in his notes after the allied invasion of Normandy. He tried to avoid capitulation to the Red Army as long as possible in order to afford German troops and civilians retreat to the west. On 7 May 1945 he signed the unconditioned surrender of the German Armed Forces to the West allied Forces in Reims.

Jodl was sentenced to death by the International Military Court and was executed on 16 October 1946. Posthumously in 1953, a West German denazification court released him from all war crimes.

8
Residential House
of Alfred Jodl

⌂ 1937 → Urbanweg, Stanggaß,
Map B 2 Colonel General Alfred Jodl met
Hitler as early as 1923 and quickly
moved up the hierarchy of the Reich
military in its preparations for war from
1933 on. Appointed Chief of the Army
headquarters in the Supreme Command
of the German Armed Forces in 1939,
he was Hitler's constant companion.
After the victorious battle against France,
he soon became the closest adviser of
the "Führer" on all war questions. As
Hitler frequently resided on Obersalzberg,
parallel with the construction of the
▷ Reich Chancellery, Berchtesgaden
Office, residences for Jodl and for
General Field Marshal Wilhelm Keitel
were built as well.
Altogether Jodl briefed Hitler during more
than 5,000 strategy discussions about
front developments, mostly in the "Wolfsschanze", the headquarter of the "Führer"
near Rastenburg in East Prussia, but also
on Obersalzberg. Far away from reality,
which became less and less favourable
from 1942, the devoted soldier took
Hitler's commands, advised, improved

and passed them on to the troops. Still,
he was the only one to have the courage
to contradict Hitler every now and then.
As the one who had all war information
coming together and who held meetings
with Hitler for hours on end, Jodl testi-
fied **"never to have heard of an annihilation of the Jews"** in June 1946.
Contradicting this statement were his
nephew's reports to him during the war,
as an eyewitness of the killing of Jews
near Minsk. Besides this, in September
1943 Jodl had addressed the German
Armed Forces in writing concerning the
deportation of the Jewish population in
Denmark.
He was thus in no way as unknowing
as he later claimed. He had known
Hitler's intentions first-hand and had
not taken action. He even considered
the members of the opposition group
around Claus von Stauffenberg as trai-
tors.
His modest residence in Stanggaß
immediately next to the Reich Chancellery served the 101st US Airborne
Division as housing after the war, among
other uses. Today the building stands
empty and is the property of the Federal
Republic of Germany.

7 Former Reich Chancellery, Berchtesgaden Office, 2005

9 Former Residential House of Wilhelm Keitel, 2005

8 Former Residential House of Alfred Jodl, 2005

9
Residential House of Wilhelm Keitel

→ Urbanweg, Stanggaß, Map B2

General Field Marshal Wilhelm Keitel, like Colonel General Alfred Jodl, belonged to Hitler's military advisers. Right next to the ▷ **Reich Chancellery, Berchtesgaden Office** the Reich built him an elaborate residence with a view of the Kehlstein. He took each of Hitler's commands without opposition and dutifully, and sanctified many war crimes with his signature. The evidence against him was so overwhelming that his defence before the International Military Court at Nuremberg feared that the Supreme Command of the German Wehrmacht might be declared a criminal organization on the basis of his crimes alone, as the Waffen SS was. Keitel's residence in Stanggaß was impounded in May 1945 by the 101st US Airborne Division and served their commander General Taylor as headquarters. Later it was renamed "Pershing House". Today the house has been lovingly restored and is private property.

10
Hospital "Dietrich Eckart"/ Rehab Clinic at Stanggaß

⌂ Edgar Berge, 1942 → Oberkälberstein, Stanggaß, Map D2 Upon personal recommendation by Hitler, Berchtesgaden received its own regional clinic at Stanggaß in 1938. The National Socialist People's Welfare Organisation (NSV – Nationalsozialistische Volkswohlfahrt) commissioned the construction. Medical technology and hygiene facilities corresponded to the most advanced standards of the time.

The combination of regional architecture and this clinic served the Nazi propaganda as a pet model for advertising the National Socialist healthcare system. Wards with a total of 200 beds were located in a 100-metre-long main building on the south slope of the mountain. From its 1942 inauguration on, the house served as an army hospital. Civilians were only treated here after the end of the war. The building is currently vacant.

Wilhelm Keitel 1882–1946

Wilhelm Keitel was born in Helmscherode on 22 September 1882. During the First World War he served as a commander on the western front. In 1938, Hitler appointed himself "Supreme Commander of the German Armed Forces" and made Keitel Chief of the "Head of Supreme Commando of the Armed Forces" (former Ministry of War). His unconditional loyalty to Hitler earned Keitel the hatred of the corps of generals and the name **"Lakeitel"**, playing on his reputation as a lackey. After the successful western front campaign of 1940, Keitel coined the label **"Greatest Army Commander of all times"** for Hitler and was appointed General Field Marshal. Keitel initially disapproved of an attack on the Soviet Union, but bent to the command of his "Führer" and made sure commands violating human rights were carried out during the battles on the eastern front. Keitel reasoned that any concessions for hindering mass murder in Poland and the "Commissary Command" would constitute a **"crime against the German people"**. After Hitler's suicide on 30 April 1945, Keitel signed the unconditional surrender of the German Armed Forces to the Red Army in Berlin-Karlshorst on 8 May 1945 as the representative of the Dönitz government. The International Military Court at Nuremberg condemned him to death for his crimes against humanity.

11
Hotel "Berchtesgadener Hof"
⌂ 1898, Heinrich Michaelis, 1940
→ Hanielstraße 7, Map D3 Bormann requested that the Hotel Industry Company of the NSDAP acquire the "Grand Hotel and Rehabilitation Sanatorium House Auguste Victoria". Up to 1940, it was remodelled as party Guesthouse and afterwards renamed "Berchtesgadener Hof". It received its own telex facility and direct telephone connections to the Party centres in Berlin and Munich. From then on foreign dignitaries, such as the British Prime Minister Chamberlain or the Italian dictator Mussolini, who Hitler received on the ▷ **"Berghof"**, resided in the Hotel "Berchtesgadener Hof". High-ranking Nazi politicians such as the Minister of Propaganda Goebbels, Minister of Foreign Affairs von Ribbentrop, "Reichsführer SS" Himmler, as well as General Field Marshal Rommel equally descended onto this then prestigious hotel.

Hitler's sister Paula was one of the permanent guests, at Hitler's wish incognito under the name of "Mrs. Wolf". After the occupation of Berchtesgaden by the US Army in the beginning of May 1945, the capitulation negotiations with General Field Marshal Kesselring were conducted at the hotel "Berchtesgadener Hof".

Until 1995 the hotel served the US army as an Armed Forces Recreation Centre. Today the building stands empty. The expansive sun balcony, the open-air swimming pool and the guestrooms are abandoned. The surroundings arc grown over by wild vegetation, a rusty sign "To Hotel" points the way to the locked main entrance.

12
Old Cemetery
⌂ 1685 → Baumgartenallee, Map E2
The old Berchtesgaden cemetery was ceremonially opened in the year of 1685. Prominent personalities found their final resting place here, such as the poster and graphic artist Ludwig Hohlwein, the writers Richard Voß and Alexander Mendelssohn-Bartholdy. Also Anton Adner, Bavaria's oldest citizen who died in 1822 at the age of 117, has his grave on this historical cementary. King Maximillian I of Bavaria donated his grave. Infamous contemporaries too ended their way through life in this cemetery, among them Dietrich Eckart, the Nazi lyricist and publisher.

Eckart had been one of the closest friends and mentors of Hitler during the 20s. Severely ill, he escaped from the 1923 Munich Putsch attempt and succumbed to a heart attack shortly afterwards. In recognition of his dubious services to "National Socialism" he received a pompous funeral celebration. His tombstone stands out like a monolith from the wooden crosses around it. Inlaid memorial plaques in the cemetery wall commemorate countless Berchtesgaden ▷ **Mountain Infantry** who paid for Hitler's wars of aggression with their young lives, far away from home.

In the Bergfriedhof cemetery on Oberschönauer Straße is Hitler's sister Paula's grave. After the early death of their parents, and besides a half-brother, she was Hitler's only living relative. According to her brother's will, she resided under a false name at the ▷ **Hotel "Berchtesgadener Hof"** from 1936 on. She died in 1960.

13
Town Hall and War Memorial
⌂ 1875 → Schlossplatz, Map E2
The facade of the Berchtesgaden Town Hall shows a memorial for the German soldiers who lost their lives in the First World War. The mural was created by the painter Josef Hengge, who also exhibited during Nazi times in Munich in the House of the German Art. Various scenes depict the themes of departure, battle, triumph, and sadness of soldiers and their families. The centre shows a large crucifix with the years 1914 and 1918.

After the Second World War, the years 1939 and 1945 were added.

The depiction of a German infantryman triumphing over Russian soldiers in winter coats was painted over in 1952.

11 "Berchtesgadener Hof", 2005

12 Old Cemetery

11 "Berchtesgadener Hof", 2005

12 Tombstone

13 Town Hall with War Memorial

12 Grave plaque of Mendelsohn-Bartholdy

15 Former SS Guardhouse, now a Gift Shop

15 Former SS Guardhouse at the Schießstättbrücke

14
Residential House and Studio of Ludwig Hohlwein
→ Schießstättstraße, Map F2

Ludwig Hohlwein had become famous as poster artist at the beginning of the 20th century and came to Berchtesgaden in the summer of 1944. Shortly after he, his daughter and grandchild managed to escape the intensifying bombing raids on Munich, his studio on Gabelsbergerstraße was destroyed during an Allied air raid. He and his family found shelter in the Berchtesgaden Artists' Home at the beginning of September 1944, which was then situated in the royal castle.

After the arrival of the US troops Hohlwein, who had also created propaganda posters for the Nazis, was prohibited to exercise his profession. He was exceptionally permitted to create a few sports and movie posters for the American Special Service.

From 24 February 1946 on, Hohlwein was permitted to work officially again. His considerable wealth, however, remained impounded.

In March 1946 he and his family moved into the "House Sonnwend" on Schießstättstraße. The new abode offered extra space for a small studio.

Hohlwein later joined the Berchtesgaden Art Guild without any political difficulties. While he participated in exhibitions, he still did not feel honoured enough as an artist in post-war Germany, despite his Nazi past. Nonetheless, he received many accolades at his 75th birthday on 27 July 1949.

Two months later, on 15 September, Hohlwein died. Together with his wife Léonie he is buried in the ▷ **Old Cemetery.** His former house is now private property.

15
SS Guardhouse I/Gift Shop "Geschenk Ladl"
⌂ 1937 → Schießstättbrücke, Map F2

The outer security zone around Hitler's ▷ **"Berghof"** started in Berchtesgaden. At the bridge Schießstättbrücke, Salzbergstraße intersects with Berchtesgadener Ache and leads steeply up to the Obersalzberg. At the bottom of the hill a little unremarkable hut still stands today, which was a guardhouse and checkpoint for the "Leibstandarte SS Adolf Hitler". Until 1945 a wooden sculpted Reich Eagle holding a swastika with an oak-leaf wreath in its claws hung under the roof beams.

Today one can still make out the year "1937" engraved over the door. During vacation seasons, the unchanged wooden hut is now the gift shop "Geschenk Ladl" for tourists, in its original state with a few publicity signs later added to it.

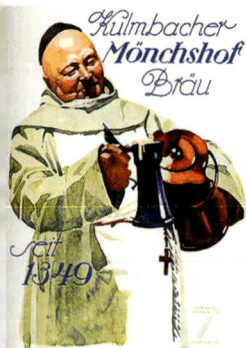

Poster Art, Publicity and Propaganda

At the beginning of the 20th century, the poster was a medium for mass communication similar to today's electronic media. Large parts of the population were influenced politically or commercially by posters. Before the professions of advertising or functional graphic designers came into existence, it was predominantly painters and architects who created posters with artistic ambitions.

Ludwig Hohlwein 1874–1949

Ludwig Hohlwein 1874–1949 Together with Lucian Bernhard, Ludwig Hohlwein was one of the most famous German poster artists. He was born in Wiesbaden on 27 July 1874. During his studies of architecture in Munich he started creating the first illustrations for the journal of the "Academic Architecture Association". Study trips led Hohlwein to London and Paris around 1900. He settled again in Munich and took commissions for the interior design of private houses, hotels and ocean liners. He regularly exhibited prints and watercolours in the Munich Glass Palace.

From 1914 on, he was one of the leading figures for the style of functional prints of his time. Even after 1918 he was able to hold this position in the booming publicity market. His perfect mastery of watercolour techniques enabled him to reproduce popular realistic motifs paired with a unique atmospheric mood. Hohlwein produced publicity, among other objects, for work tools and articles of everyday consumption including typewriters and sewing machines, cocoa, beer, tea and cigarettes, but also luxury items such as weapons and automobiles. By 1925, his repertory already included over 3,000 labels. From early on, the National Socialists had successfully vied for Hohlwein's cooperation, as they greatly admired his work. From 1932 on he worked for the NSDAP. He joined the party in 1933. The ideal of beauty of the new powers matched his own ideas of aesthetics. Some of the most effective propaganda posters thus came into existence. They focused on works for the "League of German Maidens" (BDM), the "Hitler Youth" (HJ), the Olympic Games of 1936, or the Reich Air Raid Protection Association. They all propagated the "new human": Arian, blond, sportive, heroic and distant, hardened by Nazi doctrine.

Due to his activities for the Hitler regime, Hohlwein's activities as an artist were limited during post-war times. He died on 15 September 1949 and was buried in the ▷ **Old Cemetery** in Berchtesgaden.

Hitler in Salzburg during an election campaign, 6 April 1938

SURROUNDINGS AND SALZBURG The areas around Berchtes-gaden also felt Hitler's presence on Obersalzberg. The grounds around Ainring were massively changed for the new Chancellor's own government airfield. The junction to the German highway at the nearby Walserberg border crossing was to be marked with a huge monument. After Austria was annexed, the many Austrian Nazis in Salzburg too openly confessed to their new world view. On 30 April 1938, Mozart's town of birth witnessed the one burning of books in Austrian history.

1
"Dietrich-Eckart-Haus"/ Hinterbrand Lodge
⌂ 1903 → Scharitzkehlstraße 40, Berchtesgaden, Map C4 In 1903 Countess Caroline of Ortenburg had a summer residence constructed for herself in Hinterbrand near the Hohen Göll. Because she was the first woman to climb the 2,522-metre mountain she named the seat "Göllhaus". After the countess had died, the building was rarely used until 1923 when Dietrich Eckart alias "Dr. Hoffmann" of Munich appeared on the scene to hide here from the police. Eckart was a nationalistic journalist and lyricist as well as an early supporter and mentor of Hitler. He had joined the radical rightwing "Thule Society" in 1913, the germ cell from which the NSDAP later emerged. As editor of the weekly journal "Auf gut Deutsch" (In Good German) he sharply attacked the Weimar Republic in the 20s and fanned the flames of rampant anti-Semitism. He created the expression **"Germany awaken!"** which would later decorate the flags of the NSDAP. As editor in chief of the "Völkischer Beob-achter", Eckart was temporarily arrested in the wake of Hitler's failed putsch of 9 November 1923. Afterwards he escaped seriously ill to the Göllhaus in Berchtes-gaden. On 26 December 1923 the writer died of a heart attack due to a history of alcohol and drug abuse. The Nazis gave him a pompous funeral at the ▷ **Old Cemetery.** The Göllhaus was renamed "Dietrich-Eckart-Haus" in his honor and acquired by Bormann in 1942 for the NSDAP as a Guesthouse of the ▷ **Hotel**

"Platterhof". After the war, the US army occupied the house and used it until 2004 as a convalescence home under the name of "Hinterbrand Lodge".

2
Reich Airport Reichenhall-Berchtesgaden/Bavarian Police Force Training Institution
⌂ Georg Adlmüller, 1940 → Salzburger Straße 23, Ainring, Map B1 **"Hitler over Germany"** was proudly announced in the Nazi propaganda in 1932, when Hitler carried out his election campaign by airplane. The value of rapid air transportation was quickly seized upon and after the new Chancellor had acquired the ▷ **"Berghof"** on Obersalzberg, he needed an airport nearby. It is said that Hitler himself discovered the free field as he flew over the area at Ainring three kilometres South of Freilassing. The grounds were quickly flattened and given the new undercover name "Sports Air Field" on 7 October 1933. At the request of Reich Aviation Minister Hermann Göring, the cross-Germany flight that took place in 1934 was extended to the "Führer's" new home in Berchtesgaden.
The 70 participating aircraft made a stopover in Ainring, then flew in formation toward the turn-around mark on Obersalzberg.
On 6 October 1934, the official inauguration was celebrated for this Reich Airport which, henceforth and exclusively, was to serve Nazi party officials of the highest ranks and foreign dignitaries. The showcase piece was the Flight Administration Building "Führerhaus" in the typical rural Alpine style with a representative "Führer

Reich Airport in Ainring

Room", an airport restaurant, a terrace café and an open-air swimming pool. A walkway led to the large hangar, a modern construction on steel supports.

In the course of the war, Ainring became the home airbase of the German Air Force and, with its "German Research Institute for Glider Aviation", an important base for weapons research. Between 6 and 8 July 1944 Hitler viewed a presentation of the latest infantry weapons on the airfield. Numerous high-ranking military and political representatives attended, including the Minister of Armament Speer, his second man Saur, "Reichsführer SS" Himmler, General Field Marshal Keitel, and General Guderian. The Sales Director of Mercedes-Benz, Jakob Werlin, was also present, as was the VW designer Ferdinand Porsche. Porsche developed numerous war devices on commission by the Ministry of Armament, including the VW truck and various tanks.

From the beginning of April 1945 on, airplanes from Berlin landed incessantly at Ainring and unloaded members of the Reich government as well as leaders of the German armed forces, all seeking refuge in the ▷ **Alpine Fortress.** New devices were stationed on the airfield, including new variations of Messerschmitt Me 262 jet fighters and of the ▷ **Mountain Infantry** transportation helicopter Focke-Achgelis Fa 223.

Despite all this, units of the US Army were able to capture the airfield at Ainring without any combat on 4 May 1945.

Deutschlandflug 1938
22. - 29. MAI

2 Hitler's Focke-Wulf 200 Condor on the airfield in Ainring, 1942

2 Weapons display with Speer, Hitler and Saur in Ainring

2 Former "Führerhaus" in Ainring, 2005

Preserved buildings of the airport, such as the former "Führerhaus" are now used by the Bavarian Police Institute of Continuing Education.

3
Kleßheim Castle, Guesthouse of the "Führer" / Salzburg Casino

⌂ Johann Bernhard Fischer von Erlach, 1731, Otto Strohmayr, Otto Reitter, 1942 → Kleßheimer Straße 22, Wals-Siezenheim, Map B1 Within sight of the historical part of Salzburg at the edge of a huge park is Kleßheim Castle, the best-known profane Baroque ensemble of the Salzburg region. Archbishop Johann Ernest Graf Thun commissioned the castle around 1700 from the architect of the Viennese Schönbrunn Palace, Johann Bernhard Fischer von Erlach. The main tract with the grand ballroom forms the centre of the edifice.

The castle became the "Führer's" Guesthouse in 1940 and was changed profoundly through numerous transformations and extensions. Albert Speer declared that the ensemble should stand **"in the living service of the nation because Salzburg has become so to speak the reception room for the Reich, where the people of the world (...) gather as guests".**

A three-metre-high stone Reich Eagle holding a globe in its claws still crowns each guardhouse on both sides of the gate. Shelter facilities, a private highway access, and a nearby reception railway station completed the laborious construction enterprise.

During the war against the Soviet Union Kleßheim Castle played a key role for the anti-Bolshevistic politics of the "Third Reich". As the centre of political and military coordination with his allies, this was the site at which Hitler and Reich Foreign Minister von Ribbentrop received the top representatives of the South and East European vassal states. Those who received their orders here included Benito Mussolini (Italy), Jozef Tiso (Slovakia), Ante Pavelic (Croatia), Ion Antonescu (Rumania), and Miklós

Bachem "Natter"

"Miracle Weapons" for Hitler

From 1940 on, the Reich airport grounds at Ainring housed the "German Institute for Glider Aviation" in a large collection of Barracks. The modest name camouflaged one of the most modern research facilities of the German Air Force. Here, Walter Georgii directed the construction activities of numerous excellent engineers and scientists, including the space pioneer Eugen Sänger and their future-oriented jet engine facilities and "miracle weapons" for Germany's "final victory". Besides huge transportation devices such as the Messerschmitt Me 321 "Gigant", commissioned by Hitler for the planned invasion of England, developments concentrated on prototypes of novel jet engines.

In the face of German defeat and the paucity of raw materials, the "project" division developed curious flying devices from 1943 on, such as the Bachem "Natter". This rocket-powered interception aircraft started vertically from a tower. Its belly harboured up to 34 rockets to intercept Allied bombers. After its fuel was exhausted, the pilot had to parachute out of the plane. The reusable jet engine detached simultaneously from the simple wood and metal construction and sailed to earth on a parachute. In February 1945 "Natter" was the first manned rocket to be launched. Spurred on by party offices, the industry and the military, the researchers of the DFS developed numerous future-oriented technologies, for instance the autopilot, which is still used in today's aviation.

8 Fortress Hohensalzburg on the Mönchsberg

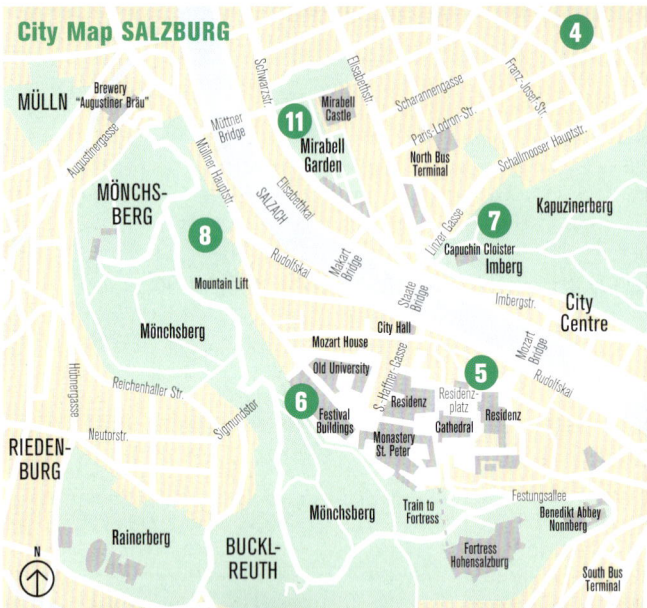

City Map SALZBURG

MÜLLN — Brewery "Augustiner Bräu"

4

Schwarzstr.

Elisabethstr.

Scharannengasse

Franz-Josef-Str.

11 Mirabell Castle

Müllner Bridge

Mirabell Garden

Paris-Lodron-Str.

North Bus Terminal

Schallmooser Hauptstr.

Augustinergasse

Müllner Hauptstr.

MÖNCHS-BERG

Elisabethkai

SALZACH

Kapuzinerberg

7 Capuchin Cloister
Imberg

8

Rudolfskai

Makart Bridge

Linzer Gasse

Imbergstr.

City Centre

Mountain Lift

State Bridge

City Hall

Mozart Bridge

Mönchsberg

Mozart House

Old University

5

Rudolfskai

Hünergasse

Reichenhaller Str.

Neutorstr.

Sigmundstor

6 Festival Buildings

S.-Haffner-Gasse

Residenz

Residenz-platz

Residenz

RIEDEN-BURG

Monastery St. Peter

Cathedral

Rainerberg

BUCKL-REUTH

Mönchsberg

Train to Fortress

Festungsallee

Benedikt Abbey Nonnberg

N

Fortress Hohensalzburg

South Bus Terminal

3 Discussing strategies with Hitler at Kleßheim Castle

3 Visit of Ante Pavelic to Kleßheim Castle, 1943

3 Foreign Minister v. Ribbentrop at Kleßheim Castle

Salzburg under the Swastika

Horthy (Hungary). In April 1943 Horthy met up with Hitler again at Kleßheim Castle. He was demanded to either kill or deport to concentration camps the 750,000 Hungarian Jews hitherto left unscathed by the Holocaust. Then, in March 1944, German troops invaded Hungary, while Horthy was detained at Kleßheim Castle. Adolf Eichmann's coordination for murdering the Hungarian Jews started immediately. For the time after the end of the Second World War, after the "final victory" for which he hoped, Hitler had selected Kleßheim Castle as the site for signing his peace treaties with his enemies, the losers of the war. History proved him wrong.

4
Synagogue

⌂ 1893 → Lasserstraße 8, Salzburg, Map C1 The first people of Jewish faith came to Salzburg in the wake of roman legionaries at a time when the city was still called "Juvavum". Historical documents show that in 1370 a prayer house and a Synagogue had their place in the current building at number 15 Judengasse. From century to century, periods of peaceful coexistence were repeatedly succeeded by anti-Semitism and expatriation of Jewish people. The Synagogue still standing today at number 8 Lasserstraße was built in 1893.
After Austria's "annexation" on 12 March 1938, German troops marched into Salzburg. The Nazis had many Jewish people arrested and confiscated their belongings of value. Even the wearing of national attire such as dirndl dresses and lederhosen was prohibited by law to "non-Arians".
In Salzburg, the "Reich Crystal Night" from 9 to 11 November 1938 did not have the effect the new men in power had desired. Jewish shops and the Synagogue were destroyed and plundered by SA men, and 71 Jewish men were arrested and deported to Dachau concentration camp, as a matter of fact. However, the jubilations of the Nazi press

about the "storm of protest by the population" were not shared by the "Security Service" of the SS. A secret internal report read: **"Due to insufficient propaganda, the population knew nothing of the deal and had no part in the actions against Jews."**
On 12 November 1938, the district leader Friedrich Rainer announced the "model region Salzburg" to be "clean of Jews". The destroyed Synagogue became property of the police department. The Jewish cemetery in Aigen was sold. Apartments and houses of deported Jews or of those who had managed to flee, including Max Reinhardt's Leopoldskron Castle, were occupied by local Nazi functionaries.
Today, Salzburg has a Jewish community once again. The Synagogue on Lasserstraße is now its religious centre as it was in the past.

5
Residenzplatz

→ Residenzplatz, Salzburg, Map C1
On 10 May 1933, the Nazis set the scene for a nationwide book burning. Under the motto **"German students march against the un-German spirit!"** student associations destroyed the works of Marxist, pacifist and Jewish writers and of authors branded as "decadent". Writings by Albert Einstein, Franz Kafka, Thomas Mann, Erich Maria Remarque, and H. G. Wells were thrown into the flames.

Until 1938, Austria had been saved from such terror. With the "annexation" to the German Reich this changed. In Salzburg, on 30 April 1938, the only book burning in Austria took place. The initiator of the spectacle was the writer and director of the "National Socialist Teachers' Association" Karl Springenschmid. Members of the "Hitler Youth" threw works of Jewish authors into the fire on Residenzplatz – among others those of Sigmund Freud, Arthur Schnitzler, Stefan Zweig and Franz Werfel, as well as those of republican pen.

8 Salzburg under the swastika, postcard of 1937 with view of Fortress Hohensalzburg

7 Sketch of the planned Regional Fortress (left), view from Mirabell Castle, 1942

6
Small Festival House
⌂ 1926 → Residenzplatz, Salzburg, Map C1 The Nazis' plans foresaw Salzburg, with its grandiose Alpine countryside and its festivities, as a kind of spa and culture region of the German Reich. In the spirit of the "Arianization" in 1938, the Salzburg festival presented itself in a changed form and with new contents. Max Reinhardt's rendering of "Faust" had to disappear along with its genial producer and the founder of the festival itself. The traditional presentation of "Jedermann" on the cathedral square was prohibited. Only Mozart and similar composers of the Baroque and Classical periods were permitted.

From 4 September 1938 on, the Festival House exhibited other forms of modern art tarnished with the label of "degenerate art". This propaganda exhibit attracted a total of 40,000 visitors. The travelling exhibit was shown throughout Germany and displayed 650 confiscated works of art by artists including Max Ernst, Paul Klee, and Otto Dix, which clashed with the Nazis' aesthetic ideals. The artists themselves were banned from carrying out their profession, were persecuted, and their names smeared. As a fringe event, the Lifka Movie Theatre in Salzburg played the movie **"The Eternal Jew"** – an anti-Semitic "documentary" about world Jewry.

Since 1945, of course, the Festival lists among its activities the works defamed between 1938 and 1945.

7
District Forum Salzburg
⌂ Otto Strohmayr, Otto Reitter, 1943 → Imberg / Kapuzinerberg, Salzburg, Map C1 As part of a major urban construction project, the District Forum of the city of Salzburg was to be built on the Imberg as a new party, cultural, educational and sports centre. The project sketches planned a big meeting hall in place of the Capuchin monastery, which was to be demolished. A square in front of it surrounded by arcades was to host service buildings for the district leader and for the NSDAP headquarters. In addition to a large sports forum,

10 Hitler and Fritz Todt on Walserberg, 1938

5 Book burning on Residenzplatz, 1938

8 Model of the planned General Command Buildings on the Mönchsberg

a new festival house was planned to stand on elevated grounds. The jewel of the whole project was to be the replacement of the Franziskischlössl with a monumental "Nazi Order Fort" with a "Führer School" for the next generation of party members. The conception had evolved in detail in 1942 up to the shape of the grounds and the walls. The megalomaniacal District Forum, however, remained unachieved, like so many other major Nazi construction projects.

8
General Command of the Army District XVIII

⌂ Heeresbauamt, 1941 → Mönchsberg, Salzburg, Map C1 City-wide constructions for a new face of Salzburg by the NS Regional Administration focused on the ▷ **District Forum** on the Kapuzinerberg and on the General Command of the Army District XVIII on the Mönchsberg, as symbols of the rulers in power, the party and the army. In the final picture if completed as planned, the medieval fortress Hohensalzburg, which had dominated the city until then, would

have looked shrunk and insignificant among the new monumental constructions.

The multi-storey General Command of the 2nd Mountain Infantry Division of the Army District XVIII and the adjoining Army Academy would have stretched over a length of 400 metres along the northern plateau of the Mönchsberg.

The administrative machinery of the Army District had been transferred to Salzburg during the early summer of 1938. This made Salzburg, after Vienna, the second most important military centre in Austria. Of all the planned buildings, only apartments and exclusive villas for officers were completed.

9
Salzburg Regional Clinic/ Hospital "Christian-Doppler", Salzburg Regional Neuroclinic

→ Ignaz-Harrer-Straße 79, Salzburg, Map C1 In the afternoon of 16 April 1941, the pale grey buses of the "Charitable Ambulance Ltd" appeared on the grounds of the Regional Clinic Salzburg for the first time. The windows

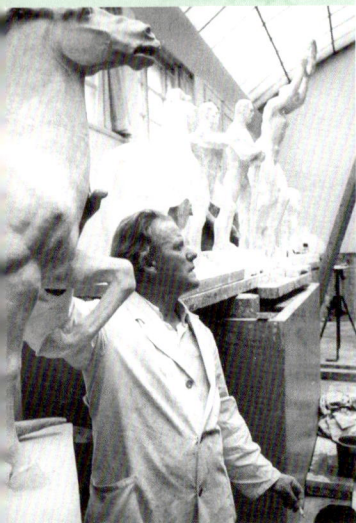

Josef Thorak 1889–1952

Josef Thorak, born in Salzburg on 7 February 1889, was the most famous sculptor of the "Third Reich" along with Arno Breker. After his studying art in Vienna and Berlin, he first worked as a freelance sculptor. He received the National Award of the Prussian Academy of Arts in 1928. From 1933 on, he was commissioned with numerous major works, predominantly by Hitler's architect Albert Speer. Thorak thus became one of the most important representatives of Nazi aesthetics and created dozens of group sculptures celebrating heroism, force, and power as new ideal of art. Among his works are various sculptures for the new Reich Chancellery and the Reich Sports Field in Berlin, the Party Conference Centre in Nuremberg, and for the world exhibit in Paris. He also created a relief for the Atatürk Monument in Ankara, as well as busts of Adolf Hitler and Benito Mussolini. Speer had his own national studio constructed for him and his monumental sculptures, including the ▷ **Monument of Work** in Salzburg, in Baldham near Munich in 1941.

Josef Thorak died in 1952. He was buried on the Salzburg cemetery of St. Peter. On his grave stands a pieta, which he completed himself.

were covered with dark sheets. The clinic personnel had already informed 68 female patients that they were to be "transferred due to the war". Transports, initially, went to Linz to the Niedernhart hospital, before the women were brought to Hartheim Castle the next day, which bore the cynical name of "convalescence home". It was in fact a place of death, an institution for the annihilation of human beings. The victims had to undress. Persons with gold teeth had a cross marked on their skin. All were led to a "shower room", the gas chamber. The bodies of those murdered were burnt afterwards in the clinic's crematorium. Between 1939 and 1941, nearly 200,000 human beings were robbed of their lives within the programme of systematic killing of persons with mental illness and disabilities. This mass murder was organized by the euthanasia centre at number 4 Tiergartenstraße in Berlin (alias "T4"). The driving force behind the "T4 campaigns" of the Salzburg Regional Clinic were the director Leo Wolf and his son Heinrich, head of the "Genetic-Biological Division". Heinrich Wolf supported the murders fanatically and is said to have combed senior citizens' homes and care facilities throughout Salzburg in search of potential victims. Altogether 262 women and men from the Salzburg Regional Clinic were taken to Hartheim Castle and murdered.

A memorial in Mirabellengarten now commemorates the victims of the Nazi euthanasia programme in Salzburg.

10
Reich Highway
Munich – Salzburg – Vienna

⌂ Sager & Woerner, 1934 → Pidding/ Walserberg, Map B2 "**German workers, begin!**" were Hitler's words in Munich Ramersdorf on 21 March 1934 to announce the construction of the highway from Munich to Salzburg. The stretch was of special interest for Hitler himself, because it considerably shortened the time to Obersalzberg on the way to Berchtesgaden. Beyond that, the provincial city of Salzburg was to be upgraded to a European cultural metropolis by

Monument of Work

way of the stretch connecting it to the Reich highway network. Under immense efforts, up to 12,000 men worked in three shifts on this stretch. Particularly during the later annexation of Austria and the Sudetenland during the year 1938, this new rapid road turned out to be an effective route for transportation of troops and provisions.

In a big propaganda performance after the "annexation" of his home country to the "Great German Reich", Hitler repeated his ceremonious start to the works on the highway near Salzburg, beginning the extension of the stretch via Linz to Vienna on 7 April 1938.

The national sculptor Josef Thorak designed a gigantic ▷ Monument of Work, which was to stand at Walserberg. The extension of the stretch was not achieved during the Second World War.

11
Monument of Work

⌂ Josef Thorak, 1938 Pidding/Walserberg, Map B1 At the border crossings into the German Reich huge monuments were to stand at the access points to the highway. The stretch Munich to Salzburg initially ended at the Austrian border crossing Walserberg. Hitler's architect Albert Speer presented a model for this position in Munich in 1938. Two huge support stones crowned with Reich Eagles and swastikas were to flank the highway at this site. Between the two lanes a sort of altar was to hold dedication and ceremonial plaques. The "annexation" of Austria to the "Third Reich" and the obliteration of the national border rendered this portal superfluous. Therefore, on 7 April 1938 Hitler repeated his ceremonious start to the works at Walserberg in a new dedication ceremony for the new highway, which was to reach Vienna in the future. The "national sculptor" Josef Thorak designed an equally gigantic "Monument of Work" which was to commemorate the labour on the highway. His sketch for the 16-metre-high stone sculpture showed four gigantic male nudes pushing a massive granite slab uphill with great effort. The design met with Hitler's approval in 1938 and negotiations for the transport of materials started. During the war work came to a halt. Parts of the completed plaster model were destroyed in 1946. The concrete foundation for the sculpture completed before the war was covered with tar in 1970 during the construction of a new border crossing.

10 About five-metre-high model of Thorak's "Monument of Work" for the highway near Salzburg, 1938

12
General-Konrad-Barracks
of the Mountain Infantry and
Mountain Artillery

⌂ Heeresbauverwaltung, 1935, 1936
→ Nonnerstraße 23–24, Bad Reichenhall, Map A2 Due to its geographic location, Bad Reichenhall was the traditional
position of the Bavarian Mountain Infantry
who served here as border troops. After
Hitler's seizure of power, construction
of an extensive military barrack area
for Battalion III of the Mountain Infantry
(100 mountain regiment) and its leadership was initiated in the autumn of 1934.
In January 1936, the added Mountain
Infantry Barrack was also completed.
In the following years the connecting
streets were broadened to fit marching
military columns. Numerous houses and
apartments for military families of the
▷ Mountain Infantry were built in the
area. The surrounding countryside of the
Alps was no longer reserved for tourism
but also as training site for the planned
war. A mural in the reception building
of the Barracks still shows four oversized
Mountain Infantrymen in the uniform of
the former German Armed Forces. Underneath, a big German Reich Eagle keeps

watch over the entrance area. In its
claws it holds a wreath of acorn leaves
with an edelweiss flower, the symbol
of the ▷ Mountain Infantry. Today the
Armed Forces of the Federal Republic of
Germany use the Barracks and maintain
the last mule unit in Bad Reichenhall.

13
Königssee

→ Königssee, Map B4 The Berchtesgaden National Park in the southeastern
corner of Bavaria is a unique nature
preservation site. The extensive 19th-cen-
tury traveller Alexander von Humboldt
called this countryside one of the "most
beautiful on earth". Grandiose high
mountain scenery surrounds the Königssee, Germany's cleanest lake. The
western shore boasts the spectacular
2,000-metre wall of the Watzmann.

The Nazis too used this most beautiful
spot on earth. Eva Braun often came
from the nearby ▷ "Berghof" for a swim
in the Königssee during the summer
months. Hitler preferred boat trips, such
as the one to the world-renowned
St. Bartholomä peninsula. Reich Marshal
Hermann Göring had hunting on his

12 Mountain Infantry Barracks

13 Königssee

13 Hitler 1935 on the Königssee, view of St. Bartholomä

mind and had his country seat nearby. "Reichsführer SS" Heinrich Himmler had the house Schneewinkellehen fitted out for himself and his secretary Hedwig Potthast in Schönau. Before Martin Bormann incorporated the building as NSDAP property, it was owned by the Jewish art historian Rudolf Berlin. The composer Max Reger and the psychoanalyst Sigmund Freud, among others, sojourned here at times.

Martin Bormann Junior remembers that Hedwig Potthast showed him and his mother the so-called "horror chamber" during a visit in the winter of 1944. All objects in it were exclusively made from raw materials of humans murdered in concentration camps. Among them was a table standing on bones of human femurs and a lamp with a lamp shade made of human skin.

Reportedly, even an edition of Hitler's book "Mein Kampf" written on human skin was present in that room. These gruesome exhibits came from concentration camps where prisoners had to produce them.

14
External Concentration Camp Hallein/Deisl Concrete Factory

⌂ 1943 → Wiestal-Landesstraße 34, Hallein, Map D3 Besides the Gestapo and the SS, the concentration camps were among the most important support structures of the Nazi terror machinery. Until the end of the war, Germany had 22 main camps within its sphere of power, among them four death camps for annihilation and over 1,200 external camps as well as external command posts.

One of the many external camps of the Dachau Concentration Camp was in the Austrian community Hallein only a few kilometres away from Hitler's ▷ "Berghof".

Deep inside a former stone mine, surrounded by high mountain walls and guarded by dense barbed wire, up to 90 prisoners subsisted in six wooden Barracks. They were assigned mostly to the Halleiner SS military Barracks for manual labour. About 2,000 men were

14 The red triangle had to be worn on the sleeve of political prisoners in concentration camps, such as the communist Josef Pliseis

stationed there, among them also a unit of the SS mountain trooper division "Handschar" which consisted of Muslim Bosnians.

At the Taugl, the prisoners had to erect a drill ground with shooting stands and a replica of a Russian village complete with an Orthodox church for simulation attacks. The Hallein prisoners were equally exposed to the brutal practices of their guards. Frequently SS guards shot prisoners "on the run", to merit five days of special vacation in return.

One of the prisoners was Josef Plieseis, who was able to escape in 1943 and became one of the most important organizers of the antifascist resistance in the Salzkammergut. Among others, the communist Agnes Primocic had supported him. She herself had been arrested several times by the Gestapo and only barely escaped deportation to the Ravensbrück Concentration Camp near Berlin. Thanks to her temerity, 17 prisoners were able to flee from the Hallein External Concentration Camp during the last days of April 1945. A few days later on 5 May, Allied troops freed the remaining prisoners. Today a concrete factory stands on these grounds.

"One has to start when injustice occurs, because after injustice follows violence."
(Agnes Primocic, resistance fighter)

Glossary

Bundeswehr – Armed Forces of the Federal Republic of Germany
BDM (Bund Deutscher Mädel) – League of German Maidens, organization for German girls and young women, part of Hitler-Jugend (HJ), both party conformist and authority abiding organizations with Nazi ideology
DFS (Deutsche Forschungsanstalt für Segelflug) – German Institute for Glider Aviation, cover name for extensive military research by the German Air Force
Flak (Flugabwehrkanone) – anti-aircraft artillery
Gauleiter – high-ranking Nazi official, appointed by Hitler and responsible for a particular district in Germany; later also in Austria and Czechoslovakia
HJ (Hitler-Jugend) – Hitler Youth, Nazi-ideology governed organization
Leibstandarte SS – SS unit specifically charged with the protection of the "Führer"
Luftwaffe, Wehrmachtsteil – German Air Force, part of German Armed Forces including the army, navy and air force
Nazi – abbreviation for National Socialist
NSDAP (National Socialist German Workers Party) – Official name of the Nazi party
NSV (Nationalsozialistische Volkswohlfahrt) – National Socialist People's Welfare, commissioned luxurious constructions for elitist use with NSDAP funds
Nürnberg (Nuremberg) – seat of the international military tribunal against German war criminals
Oberkommando – Supreme Command
RSHA (Reichssicherheitshauptamt) – Reich Central Security Office
SS (Schutzstaffel) – originally an elite guard, which later, under Himmler, developed into a mass army and political police force
Wehrmacht – German Armed Forces

Selected Bibliography

Beierl, Florian M.: Hitlers Berg. Licht ins Dunkel der Geschichte. Die geheimen Bunkeranlagen des Obersalzberg, Berchtesgaden 2004

Benz, Wolfgang u.a. (Hg.): Enzyklopädie des Nationalsozialismus, München 2001

Benz, Wolfgang, Walter H. Pehle (Hg.): Lexikon des deutschen Widerstandes, Frankfurt am Main 1999

Chaussy, Ulrich: Nachbar Hitler. Führerkult und Heimatzerstörung am Obersalzberg, Berlin 2006

Fest, Joachim: Hitler. Eine Biographie, Frankfurt am Main 1973

Fest, Joachim: Speer. Eine Biographie, Berlin 1999

Kershaw, Ian: Hitler, Stuttgart 1998, 2000

Möller, Horst u.a. (Hg.): Die tödliche Utopie. Bilder, Texte, Dokumente, Daten zum Dritten Reich, München 2002

Nerdinger, Winfried (Hg.): Bauen im Nationalsozialismus. Bayern 1933–1945, München 1993

Seidler, Franz W.; Zeigert, Dieter: Die Führerhauptquartiere. Anlagen und Planungen im Zweiten Weltkrieg, München 2000

Weihsmann, Helmut: Bauen unterm Hakenkreuz. Architektur des Untergangs, Wien 1998

Weiß, Hermann (Hg.): Biographisches Lexikon zum Dritten Reich, Frankfurt am Main 1999

Wintersteller, Wolfgang: KZ Dachau – Außenlager Hallein, Hallein 2003

Imprint

A catalogue record for this publication
is available from the Deutsche Bibliothek
in the Deutsche Nationalbibliographie;
detailed bibliographical data are available
on the internet at http://dnb.ddb.de

First Edition, March 2007
© Christoph Links Verlag –
LinksDruck GmbH, 2005
Schönhauser Allee 36, 10435 Berlin
Tel.: +49 30 44 02 32-0

Front Cover Design: Maik Kopleck
Text / Design / Illustrations / Maps:
Maik Kopleck, STAAB/KOPLECK:DESIGN!
www.staab-kopleck-design.de

Translation: Irene Grote, Berlin
DTP: Marina Siegemund, Berlin
Printed by:
AZ Druck und Datentechnik, Kempten

ISBN 978-3-86153-422-8

Maik Kopleck

Born in 1975,
studied Commu-
nication Design at
the University of
Applied Sciences
in Düsseldorf, was freelance Art Director
with several advertising agencies in
Düsseldorf and Berlin. Then freelance
photographer in San Francisco;
co-director of the design company
STAAB/KOPLECK:DESIGN! in Düsseldorf,
founded in 1996.

Acknowledgements

Special thanks to Hans Kopleck, Brigitte
Staab, Ernst Staab, Prof. Werner Holzwarth,
Morris Aberham, Dr. Robert Kuhn, Prof.
Vilibald Barl, Lena Brombacher, Alexander
Römer, Martin Venn, Susanne Büker and
Jens Kamphausen.

Photographs

On pages with several photographs, the
sources are given from the top to the
bottom of the page and from left to right.
All photographs, maps and illustrations
without acknowledgement are from the
author or the publisher. In a few cases,
the rightful copyright owner could not
be identified and we would be pleased
to hear from them.

Archiv Reiner Janick, Verein Berliner
Unterwelten: p. 31, 38

Bayerische Staatsbibliothek München/
Bildarchiv Hoffmann: p. 2, 5 top, 7,
8/9 top, 9 bottom, 12 top, 13, 14, 16,
17, 23 top left/bottom, 37 right, 39,
41, 46, 50 bottom left/bottom right,
53 top left, 54, 56 bottom right

Dokumentationsarchiv des österreichi-
schen Widerstandes Wien: p. 53 top right

Ullstein Bild: p. 23 right, 48 middle/
left bottom

German Edition

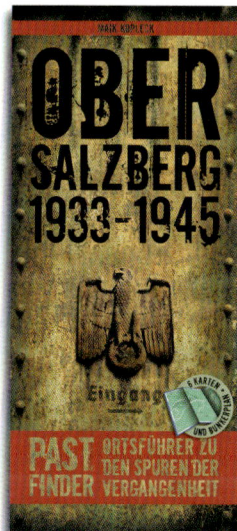

ISBN 978-3-86153-355-9

Surrounding Area and Salzburg

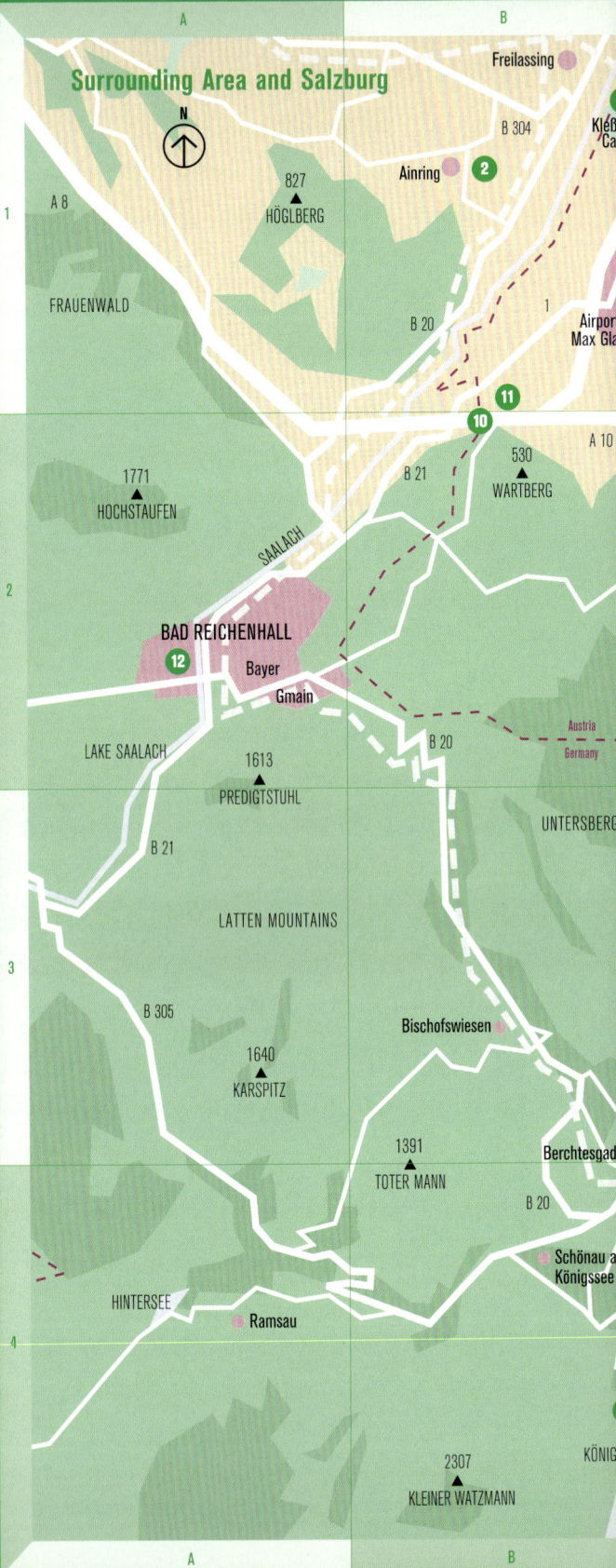

N
↑

Freilassing

KleB
Cas

B 304

A 8

Ainring ② 2

827
▲ HÖGLBERG

B 20

Airport
Max Gla

1

FRAUENWALD

⑪
⑩

A 10

1771
▲ HOCHSTAUFEN

B 21

530
▲ WARTBERG

SAALACH

2

BAD REICHENHALL
⑫

Bayer

Gmain

Austria
Germany

B 20

LAKE SAALACH

1613
▲ PREDIGTSTUHL

UNTERSBERG

B 21

LATTEN MOUNTAINS

3

B 305

1640
▲ KARSPITZ

Bischofswiesen

1391
▲ TOTER MANN

Berchtesgad

B 20

Schönau a
Königssee

HINTERSEE

Ramsau

4

2307
▲ KLEINER WATZMANN

KÖNIG

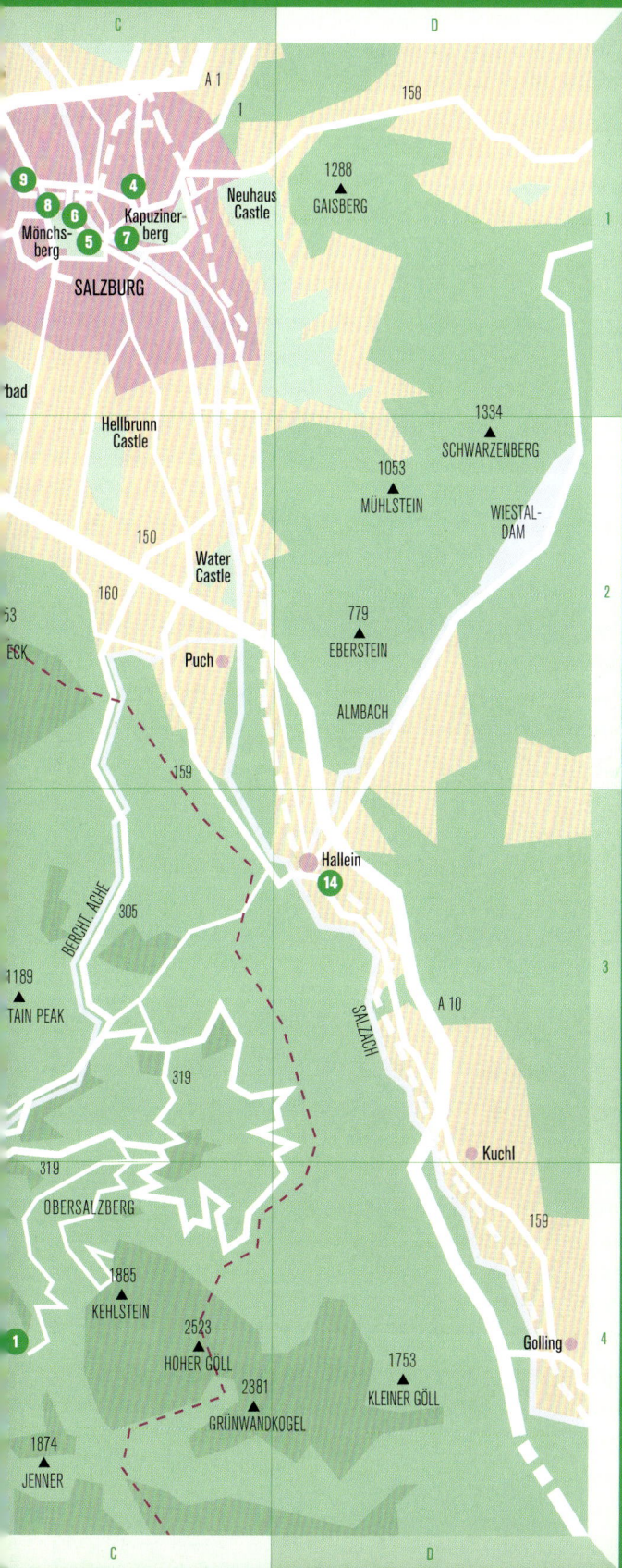

C   D

A 1
1   158

⑨   1288 ▲
  ⑧   GAISBERG
    ⑥   Neuhaus
      ④   Kapuziner- Castle
Mönchs-   ⑤   ⑦   berg
berg

SALZBURG   1

                                            1334 ▲
bad   SCHWARZENBERG

Hellbrunn
Castle   1053 ▲
                                MÜHLSTEIN   WIESTAL-
                                                 DAM
150
                   Water
              Castle
160   2
53   779 ▲
                                EBERSTEIN
ECK
             Puch ●
                                ALMBACH

         159

                             Hallein ●
                              ⑭

                                                           3
1189 ▲   A 10
TAIN PEAK

BERCHT. ACHE   305

                319

319   Kuchl ●

OBERSALZBERG   159

        1885 ▲
        KEHLSTEIN
              2523 ▲
①   HOHER GÖLL   1753 ▲   Golling ●   4
                 2381 ▲   KLEINER GÖLL
                 GRÜNWANDKOGEL
1874 ▲
JENNER

C   D

Berchtesgaden

N ↑

A

B

1

Moos

Haus Stodel

Oisler

Staatsstr. 2097

Ponn

Reittoffen

Bachinger Weg

Bachinger

Gypsmühle

Urbanweg

Tristramweg

2

9

Tristram

8 **7**

BISCHOFSWIESENER ACHE

Meisllehen

Senior Citizen's
Home "Insula"

5

Insulaweg

3

Burger

Gebirgsjägerstr.

6

Strub

B 20

Ramsauer S...

Silbergstr.

B 305

4

Stang

A

B